THE
SCOTTISH
GAELIC
TATTOO
HANDBOOK

*Authentic words and phrases
in the Celtic language
of Scotland*

by
Emily McEwan

**bradan
press**

Halifax, Nova Scotia

Bradan Press
Halifax, Nova Scotia, Canada
www.bradanpress.com
info@bradanpress.com

Disclaimer: This book is designed to provide information only. The author and publisher shall have no liability or responsibility to any person or entity regarding any loss or damage incurred, or alleged to have incurred, directly or indirectly, by the information contained in this book. Additionally, while the author and publisher have made every effort to ensure the accuracy of the information within this book at time of publication, the author and publisher do not assume and hereby disclaim any liability to any party for any loss, damage, or disruption caused by errors or omissions, whether such errors or omissions result from accident, negligence, or any other cause.

Library and Archives Canada Cataloguing in Publication

McEwan, Emily, author
     The Scottish Gaelic tattoo handbook : authentic words
and phrases in the Celtic language of Scotland / by Emily McEwan.

Includes bibliographical references and index.
Issued in print and electronic formats.
ISBN 978-0-9950998-0-7 (paperback).--ISBN 978-0-9950998-3-8
(pdf).--ISBN 978-0-9950998-2-1 (mobi).--ISBN 978-0-9950998-1-4
(epub)

     1. Scottish Gaelic language--Handbooks, manuals, etc.
2. Scottish Gaelic language--Terms and phrases--Handbooks,
manuals, etc. 3. Scottish Gaelic language--Glossaries, vocabularies
, etc.--Handbooks, manuals, etc. 4. Tattooing--Handbooks, manuals
, etc. 5. Words in art--Handbooks, manuals, etc. I. Title.

PB1514.M34 2016   491.6'3   C2016-902769-4
                                          C2016-903449-6

Front and back cover illustrations © 2016 by Pat Fish
Pat Fish is known internationally for her Celtic tattoo art, bringing the ancient illuminated manuscripts and patterns from standing stones alive in skin. View her work at www.luckyfish.com and www.luckyfishart.com.

Back cover author photo © 2016 by Rebecca Clarke, www.rebeccaclarke.ca

Figures © 2016 by Emily McEwan-Fujita

Gaelic editors:
Marcas Mac an Tuairneir, www.marcasmac.co.uk
Angus MacLeod, St. Ann's Bay, Nova Scotia, Canada

Table of Contents

Introduction   1

Chapter 1: What is Scottish Gaelic?   3

    History and current situation   3

    Brief description of the language   5

Chapter 2: Gaelic Tattoo Problems   9

    The definition of translation   9

    Inadequate translation methods   11

        Using machine translation   11

        Using an English-to-Gaelic dictionary   12

        Copying examples from the internet   13

        Asking a stranger to translate for free   13

        Asking a friend or family member   15

    Real-life examples   16

        Military service   16

        Honouring a family member   18

        Scottish nationalist sentiment   20

        Love for a partner   22

    Gaelic tattoo ethics   25

Chapter 3: How to Choose a Gaelic Tattoo   27

    Use the glossary in this book   27

    Pay a professional translator   28

    Learn the language   28

    Forewarning   29

Chapter 4: The Basics of Gaelic Writing   31

    The Gaelic alphabet   31

    Gaelic spelling rules   32

Accent marks and apostrophes   33

Which font to use   34

How to pronounce Gaelic   36

Chapter 5: Gaelic Tattoo Glossary   39

How to use the glossary   39

How to search   40

Format of entries   40

Parts of speech   40

Capitalization   41

Bible verse excerpts   42

Gaelic proverbs   42

The Gaelic Tattoo Glossary   43

Place and identity   43

Family   47

Love and friendship   54

In memoriam   59

Religious and spiritual   62

Courage, honour, and military service   66

Work, activities, and identities   68

Emotions, qualities, and concepts   71

Gaelic proverbs and expressions   75

References   79

Glossary Index   81

Introduction

People have many different reasons for getting a tattoo with a word or phrase in Scottish Gaelic. Perhaps your parents or grandparents spoke Gaelic and the language reminds you of them. Maybe your ancestors emigrated from a Gaelic-speaking area of Scotland and the language symbolizes your family history.

Many people relate to Gaelic on a symbolic level as well. If you are Scottish or of Scottish heritage, you may see Gaelic as a symbol of Scotland. Gaelic is also a Celtic language, and for many people Celtic art and culture hold great aesthetic and even spiritual appeal.

Whatever the reason you want a tattoo, you are in charge of getting it right. A good tattoo artist will advise you to do your research before you get a tattoo that incorporates words or symbols from another language or culture. For example, Pat Fish is a tattoo artist in Santa Barbara, California who specializes in Celtic design. Pat includes the following section on her release form which clients must initial:

If the tattoo has an element that is written in a language other than English, Tattoo Santa Barbara takes no responsibility for the accuracy of that text. It is the client's responsibility alone to check for the correct words and spelling or symbols.

In other words, you are solely responsible for the non-English content of your tattoo. However, finding a suitable Gaelic phrase and confirming its accuracy is not easy. In fact, getting a tattoo in a language you don't understand is risky, especially in the internet age.

Social media sites regularly share stories and photos about people with embarrassing tattoo mistakes in other languages. People have gotten tattoos with Chinese characters backwards or upside down, or ones that read "rice fried in pork fat" or "meanie crime poet."

One American man in Arkansas got a giant Hebrew tattoo on his forearm that he thought meant "strength" but actually meant "matzo," the unleavened cracker-like bread eaten at Jewish Passover celebrations. People have tried to get Christian tattoos in Hebrew that end up mangling the name of the very God they are trying to honour.

This book can save you from making similar tattoo mistakes in Gaelic. It offers real-life examples, professional linguistic insight, advice from a Gaelic-speaking perspective, and a list of ready-made translations.

This book does not contain any tattoo artwork. Once you've settled on your preferred wording, you can bring it to a tattoo artist and work with him or her to incorporate it into a design of your choice.

Readers are invited to explore the art of Pat Fish, the creator of this book's cover art. Pat's website luckyfishart.com features a wide range of Celtic art tattoo designs. Readers may use the coupon code **GAELIC1** to receive a discount on the purchase of her tattoo designs, including a version of the lion featured on the front cover.

Professionally designed tattoo images combined with an accurate Gaelic word or phrase will give you a true work of art: one uniquely suited to you, that communicates in both beautiful images and meaningful words.

Chapter 1

What is Scottish Gaelic?

For most English speakers, even basic information about Scottish Gaelic is not well understood. This chapter offers some of the most important facts to know about Gaelic before you choose to incorporate a word or phrase into a tattoo. These facts are divided into two main areas: the history and present-day situation of the language, and basic linguistic knowledge.

History and current situation

Gaelic is often called an "ancient language," but the poetic claim that it was spoken in the Garden of Eden should not be taken literally. Most scholars agree that Gaelic was first brought to Scotland from Ireland around the 4th or 5th century CE, though some scholars have argued that it may have developed much earlier, concurrently in Scotland and Ireland. Until about the 8th century, Gaelic was spoken mainly in the Kingdom of Dál Riata on the west coast. Gaelic spread throughout the western and northern areas of what became the Kingdom of Alba between 800 and 1100 CE. The Gaelic linguistic area started to shrink from the 12th century onward, and by 1400 Gaelic was no longer the main language of Scotland, although it has continued to be spoken in Scotland ever since.

At present, Gaelic is considered one of the world's "lesser-used languages," languages which are still living but are spoken by relatively smaller numbers of people.

Gaelic may seem like a mysterious language to those who are not already part of a Gaelic community. For Gaelic speakers themselves, though, the language is not mysterious; it is just a part of everyday life. It is still hidden in a sense, because of how thoroughly it was neglected and discouraged by British, Scottish, and Canadian institutions including governments, schools, the church, and ultimately many speakers themselves. The result is that in most places these days, even in Gaelic-speaking areas, one does not simply walk out the front door and hear the language. In other words, you have to know where to find Gaelic speakers and how to engage with them.

Gaelic has long been thought of as the language of rural areas in both Scotland and Nova Scotia. But Gaelic is no longer a village or community language; instead it is the language of social networks. Networks of Gaelic speakers are related to where people live, but are now based mostly on shared workplaces, educational institutions, voluntary activities, and of course online interaction.

Since 2005, Gaelic has been an official national language of Scotland. The 2011 Scottish census counted about 58,000 Gaelic speakers over the age of three in Scotland, which is 1.1% of the Scottish population of 5.1 million. Over 23,000 additional people reported that they could understand Gaelic, but not speak it, for a total of over 80,000 people with some Gaelic language ability. All Gaelic speakers of school age and older are bilingual in English and Gaelic. In Scotland, Gaelic is spoken on the west coast and the Hebridean islands, as well as in urban centres such as Glasgow, Inverness, Edinburgh, and Aberdeen.

In Canada, Gaelic was the third most commonly-spoken language after English and French at the time of Canadian confederation in 1867. Gaelic went through a similar process of decline in Canada as in Scotland, however. Gaelic still lacks any official status in Canada or its provinces, but it is spoken in the province of Nova Scotia in social networks mostly located in Cape Breton Island, Antigonish County, Pictou County, and the Halifax area. The 2011 Canadian census counted over 1200 Gaelic speakers in Nova Scotia.

In the English-speaking world, Gaelic is still very much outside of mainstream culture and media. Many people discover Scottish Gaelic language and culture for the first time through commercial music recordings, and more recently through the *Outlander* books and television series.

Brief description of the language

Several basic aspects of the Scottish Gaelic language are helpful to understand. First, Scottish Gaelic is a real, natural, human language. It is not an invented language like Tolkien's Elvish. It does not have mystical or magical properties. It is also not slang or patois. It is not gibberish, as many English speakers have claimed over the past several centuries. Scottish Gaelic has grammar, vocabulary, textbooks, dictionaries, a written literature, and an extensively documented oral literature.

Although it might seem hard to believe, some people in Scotland still despise Gaelic and want to see it disappear altogether. They denounce public funding for Gaelic. Astonishingly, a few voices in the mainstream media still disparage Gaelic on a regular basis and get away with it. If a newspaper printed the same slurs about an immigrant language or its speakers in the U.K., this would be considered racist hate speech.

The second key fact to know is that Scottish Gaelic is a Celtic language. The term "Celtic" is used in many ways, but in linguistics, Celtic is the name of a language family. The Celtic language family is part of a larger Indo-European family of languages, that also includes the Germanic, Indo-Iranian, Romance, and Slavic language families.

Six Celtic languages are spoken in the 21st century. They are divided into two branches, as shown in Figure 1. These two branches are called Brythonic (or P-Celtic) and Goidelic (or Q-Celtic) in historical linguistics. Three modern languages are included in the Brythonic branch. Breton (called *Brezhoneg* in Breton) is spoken in areas of Brittany in northwest France. Cornish (*Kernowek*) has been revived and is spoken by groups of people in Cornwall. Welsh (*Cymraeg*) is spoken in areas of Wales and also by descendants of Welsh emigrants in Patagonia, Argentina.

Categorization of Celtic Languages in *Ethnologue: Languages of the World*

Indo-European languages (444 total)
> **Celtic (6 total)**
>> Insular Celtic
>>> **Brythonic (3)**
>>>> • Breton (France)
>>>> • Cornish (UK)
>>>> • Welsh (UK)
>>> **Goidelic (3)**
>>>> • Scottish Gaelic (UK)
>>>> • Irish (Ireland)
>>>> • Manx (Isle of Man)

Figure 1: Modern Celtic languages

Of the modern languages in the Goidelic or Gaelic branch, Scottish Gaelic (called *Gàidhlig*) is spoken in areas of Scotland and Nova Scotia, Canada; Irish (*Gaeilge*) is spoken in areas of Ireland and Northern Ireland; and Manx Gaelic (*Gaelg*) has been revived and is spoken in the Isle of Man.

Like the other Celtic languages, Gaelic is a VSO language in structure. This is a language in which most sentences are arranged in the order verb-subject-object. By contrast, the majority of the world's languages are either subject-object-verb (SOV, for example, Japanese) or subject-verb-object (SVO, for example, English).

The third key fact to know about Scottish Gaelic is that it is similar to Irish. You could call Irish a sister language to Scottish Gaelic, since they both developed from the same ancestor language which is called Old Irish.

Although Scottish Gaelic and Irish are related, most Irish dialects are not mutually intelligible with Scottish Gaelic. This means that speakers of each dialect cannot understand each other very well (although usually their understanding can be improved with practice). Figure 2 uses a common sentence to illustrate some of the differences between Scottish Gaelic and Irish dialects.

The fourth key fact to understand about Scottish Gaelic is that it is a totally different language from Scots. Scots is a language that belongs to the Germanic language family, the same Indo-European language family as English. The Germanic language family also includes German, Dutch, and Afrikaans, as well as Norwegian, Danish, Swedish, Icelandic, and Faroese. Scots and English developed from the common ancestor language Anglo-Saxon (Old English).

Because Scots and English are so closely related, many English speakers can understand some Scots. All Scots speakers can understand English because they are exposed to it so frequently in the media, school, and communities. There are four main dialect regions of the Scots language in Scotland; in each of these regions, various sub-dialects are still spoken today.

"How are you?" in some dialects of Scottish Gaelic and Irish

SCOTTISH GAELIC (*Gàidhlig*)

General:	Ciamar a tha thu?
Lewis dialect:	Dè man a tha thu?

IRISH (*Gaeilge*)

Ulster dialect:	Cad é mar atá tú?
Connaught dialect:	Cén chaoi a bhfuil tu?
Munster dialect:	Conas 'tá tú?

Figure 2: Differences between Scottish Gaelic and Irish

Scots is also the language used by the poet Robert Burns in his poetry and songs, including his famous song "Auld Lang Syne" (which means "Old Long Since" or "Old Times" in English).

In contrast, as previously mentioned, the Scottish Gaelic language is in the Celtic language family. The Celtic and Germanic language families are both Indo-European, so Scottish Gaelic is related to English in that respect, but only distantly. Figure 3 compares the same sentence in English, Scots, and Scottish Gaelic to give a sense of the differences.

Some people still call the Scottish Gaelic language by the older term "Scots Gaelic." However, this term sounds too similar to the unrelated "Scots." The preferred English term for the modern Scottish Gaelic language is "Scottish Gaelic."

In summary, Scottish Gaelic is a real Celtic language which is closely related to the Irish language, and only very distantly related to the Scots and English languages. Whether you have been drawn to Gaelic through its history, music or Celtic culture, the chapters ahead will help you identify how to plan a Gaelic tattoo that avoids common problems and mistakes.

The Same Sentence in English, Scots, and Gaelic

ENGLISH
Have a happy St. Andrew's Day everybody!

SCOTS
Hae a braw St. Andra's Day awbodie!

SCOTTISH GAELIC
Là Fhèill Anndrais sona dhuibh uile!

Figure 3: English, Scots, and Scottish Gaelic comparison

Chapter 2

Gaelic Tattoo Problems

Planning a Gaelic tattoo when you do not speak the language can lead to a number of common problems. This chapter clarifies what is involved in the act of translation, describes the inadequate translation methods that people often choose, offers some real-life examples of Gaelic tattoo mistakes, and concludes with a discussion of tattoo ethics.

The definition of translation

Many people who seek a Gaelic translation of an English word or phrase for a tattoo do not fully understand the meaning of the word "translation." They have unreasonable expectations about what can be translated and do not realize how difficult translation can be.

Translation is a process of taking an original text in one written language (the "source language"), and using it to create a new text with the same or equivalent meaning as the original in a different written language (the "target language"). However, creating an equivalent meaning through translation can mean different things to different people.

There are two main types of translation, which for many centuries have been called something like "word-for-word" and "sense-for-sense."

Word-for-word or "literal" translation follows the form of the source language as closely as possible, even if it sounds unusual in the target language.

Sense-for-sense or "free" translation tries to create an overall equivalent meaning in the target language, even if words and expressions with meanings different from the source language must be used to achieve this.

Although these two concepts represent very different goals in translation, think of them as two ends of a continuum. Most translations will be found somewhere along that continuum in terms of how directly faithful they are to the source text. Keep in mind that there is no such thing as a true or perfect translation of a written text. No translation ever fully captures the sound, sense, feel, and cultural meanings of the original text.

People who request Gaelic tattoos, and well-meaning Gaelic learners who assist them, often pursue word-for-word translations from English into Gaelic. They are the easiest to do and do not require much Gaelic cultural background knowledge. However, often these literal translations do not make sense, sound beautiful, or convey culturally appropriate meanings in Gaelic, even when each individual word is translated correctly. Some of the examples later in the chapter illustrate this problem.

An entire academic field is devoted to translation studies. Numerous training programs teach people how to translate and interpret from various source languages into various target languages. Volumes have been written about the history, philosophy, and dilemmas of translation. There is no room to discuss the issues here, but anyone who requests or attempts a translation should at least be aware that translation is an art requiring detailed knowledge of both source and target languages and cultures.

Inadequate translation methods

In addition to having an overly-literal understanding of translation, people may try the following inadequate translation methods in their efforts to obtain a Gaelic tattoo translation: 1) using machine translation; 2) looking it up in a Gaelic-English dictionary; 3) copying an example from the internet; 4) asking a stranger to do it for free; and 5) asking a friend or family member. Each of these methods, as we shall see, involves unrealistic expectations of language, human beings, or computers.

Using machine translation

Many people look for a website that will automatically translate English to Scottish Gaelic. Internet search results seem to suggest that this is possible. Some of the sites that claim to offer Gaelic translation, however, only have links to dictionaries. Others have their own databases copied or stolen from dictionaries. The rest simply don't work, with one exception.

Google Translate now offers machine translation, or translation carried out by a computer, for Scottish Gaelic. However, you cannot rely on Google Translate to give you an accurate translation for a tattoo. Sometimes it can be useful for giving a general idea of the meaning of a word or phrase. But informal experiments with English-to-Gaelic in Google Translate indicate that it rarely gives accurate or grammatically correct results. Google Translate also cannot handle idioms, phrases whose overall meaning is not the same as the literal meaning of the words.

The service is unlikely to improve over time. Google Translate has been available for Irish since 2009 but it is still completely unreliable. When companies and governments use Google's Irish translations on signs and in official documents, embarrassing mistakes can result.

Human language is so complex that machine translation needs a number of special conditions to work well—and those conditions are unavailable for Scottish Gaelic right now. Michael Bauer, a Gaelic IT specialist, says these requirements would include "a massive (billions of words) aligned bilingual corpus," which is to say, a data set including a huge number of documents already translated from English to Gaelic or vice versa. A collection of parallel texts this large does not exist. One could theoretically create it, but the funding to do so is currently lacking. The future provision of high-quality Gaelic-English machine translation services by private companies or governments is highly unlikely. Gaelic is an endangered language with relatively few speakers and limited financial resources. Legally, politically, or financially, Gaelic is not supported by the Scottish, UK, or EU governments to the same extent that Irish is supported by Ireland and the EU.

The most successful machine translation involves source and target languages that are structurally similar, as Bauer also points out. Machine translation works fairly well between Irish, Scottish Gaelic, and Manx Gaelic, which are all in the same branch of the Celtic language family (see the website www.intergaelic.com). However, Scottish Gaelic and English are very different from each other which makes quality machine translation vastly more difficult to achieve.

Even if prepared with a massive data input, however, machine translation would still only work well for translating short phrases and sentences that are literal in meaning. Many of the phrases and quotes that people want for tattoos cannot be translated by machines because they are complex, metaphorical, culturally-specific, and artistic.

Using an English-to-Gaelic dictionary

In the absence of science fiction devices like the Babel fish of *The Hitchhiker's Guide to the Galaxy* or the TARDIS translation circuit of Doctor Who, some people search for an online English–Gaelic dictionary to look up a phrase they want to use in their tattoo. This approach also poses problems, however, because Gaelic has a very different grammatical system from English. Looking up the Gaelic for each individual word in an English phrase, and then stringing those Gaelic words together in English order, will almost never result in a good translation because the way that words are combined into expressions in Gaelic is rarely the same as in English.

In addition, the spelling and pronunciation of Gaelic words often change when they are combined into phrases and sentences. A Gaelic dictionary provides some information about this, but before you can use a dictionary accurately for translation, you need an understanding of the grammatical rules of Gaelic.

Copying examples from the internet

Some people are tempted to use a translation that they find on the internet, whether in Wikipedia or in a photo of another person's tattoo, jewelry, or a t-shirt for sale. However, just because you see something in Gaelic on Wikipedia, Buzzfeed, Pinterest, Zazzle, or Etsy, you cannot be confident that it is correct.

A lot of information on the internet is copied and re-circulated which spreads and perpetuates mistakes. Therefore, when using Gaelic examples from the internet, be aware of whether the source is a reputable Gaelic institution or individual.

Asking a stranger to translate for free

Many people look for a discussion forum, Facebook group, or blog where they can request a free tattoo translation from a stranger. While asking a human being is a better idea than asking a computer, there are still many limitations and ethical issues to consider with this approach.

Many adults learning Gaelic are not yet fluent in the language or knowledgeable enough about the culture to attempt translations. They may be enthusiastic about helping, but a little knowledge can be dangerous when paired with overconfidence. If you are lucky, with their help you may end up with a translation that is literally correct. However, even a literally correct translation may sound strange and un-Gaelic to fluent Gaelic speakers. More often than not, this is because the exact thing you want your tattoo to say is not ever actually said in Gaelic. Just because something can be literally translated does not mean that the results will sound good or make cultural sense.

I cannot overemphasize how many requests for translations of this type are received by Gaelic speakers and organizations on a regular basis. Most fluent Gaelic speakers are polite about the avalanche of free tattoo requests they receive, even when they are frustrated. The vast majority of Gaelic speakers would not lead you astray by giving you a fake translation. However, are you willing to risk the possibility, especially if you plan to share photos of your tattoo online with the rest of the world?

Even when fluent speakers are assisting you, they may disagree on the best way to translate your request. Thus if you are seeking free assistance on a forum where the policy allows it, and members are willing to help, you should still wait until more than one person has agreed on a translation before considering it safe to proceed with a tattoo. The Irish Language Forum, which handles requests for Irish tattoo translations, advises waiting until at least three regulars have weighed in and agreed on a translation.

Sometimes there will be lively discussion about a translation, but no easy agreement. Translation involves not only skill and knowledge, but also the art of interpretation. For entertainment, a friend of mine recently asked his Facebook friends how they would translate Captain Jean-Luc Picard's signature phrase "Make it so!" from the television series "Star Trek: The Next Generation." The friends, all fluent Gaelic speakers, came up with eleven different suggestions (which I have back-translated):

- *Biodh amhlaidh!* (Let it be in this manner!)
- *Biodh e mar seo!* (Let it be like this!)
- *Cuir an gnìomh e!* (Apply it!)
- *Cuir air dòigh e!* (Arrange it!)
- *Cuir saod air!* (Arrange it!)
- *Dall ort!* (Go on!)
- *Dèan e!* (Do it!)
- *Dèan mar sin e!* (Do it like that!)
- *Siuthad ma-tha!* (Go on then!)
- *Steall ort a mheat!* (Full speed, mate!)
- *Thoir gu buil e!* (Accomplish it!)

Some of these options sound more serious, others more humorous. Some sound like requests, others like orders. Some sound more literal and English, others more culturally Gaelic. They are all legitimate attempts at translation, but not one of them has the same unique feel to it as Captain Picard's original catchphrase.

A legitimate translation of this phrase would involve many resources and much cooperation. If the entire ST:TNG series were translated for Gaelic television (a Gaelic Trek fan's dream, but sadly unlikely), then a new translation for that phrase would be agreed upon by a team of writer-translators, in the context of many other translation decisions about the portrayal of characters, and probably through long debates over numerous cups of tea. The translated phrase would then take on the connotations of ST:TNG and Captain Picard for Gaelic-speaking viewers as it was viewed in the context of each episode and season. But one English speaker cannot create that communal social and cultural meaning with a one-off tattoo translation.

This example illustrates the fact that translating catch phrases, jokes, poetry, and song lyrics is challenging for fluent speakers and not an enterprise to be undertaken lightly. The longer, more elaborate, or context-specific your request is, the harder it will be to translate.

Asking a friend or family member

If you are lucky enough to know someone who studies Gaelic, you could ask them for a translation. But unless your friend or family member is a fluent speaker or Gaelic teacher, then for the sake of your relationship it may be best not to ask them for a translation of anything more complicated than a word or two. Most adults who are learning Scottish Gaelic are not at the skill level of a professional translator.

One final point that you may never have considered is the question of how well a Gaelic speaker can write and spell Gaelic. There are many people who have some Gaelic language skills, but not enough to easily translate and spell a tattoo request. Let's take Scotland, where the most Gaelic speakers live, as an example. The 2011 Scottish census counts the Gaelic language abilities of everyone over the age of three, but if we think about the Gaelic users who could realistically help you with a tattoo translation request, perhaps they would be the ones aged 18–84. In this broad age group, there are 73,204 people who say they have some Gaelic ability. But of this total:

- over 17,000 say they can speak Gaelic, but *cannot read or write it*;

- over 21,000 say they can understand Gaelic, but *cannot speak, read, or write it*;

- over 5,500 say they can speak and read Gaelic, but *cannot write it*;

- over 4,400 say they can read Gaelic but *cannot speak or write it*.

That's over 46,000 people, well over half of the adults in Scotland aged 18–84 with Gaelic ability, who are not fully literate in the language—and therefore cannot guarantee you a correctly-spelled tattoo.

Don't blame them. The reason that many of these folks can't write Gaelic is because they were not provided with a school education in Gaelic. Most of them probably never had formal Gaelic grammar lessons or spelling instruction. The rest are still in the process of learning the language.

You may be shocked at these statistics, but this is a typical situation for a minority language community where children are only guaranteed to receive schooling in the majority language, not necessarily in the minority language. People who grew up in families that speak nothing but English don't often think about what it would be like to be able to have a conversation but not to be able to read books or write an e-mail in a language. You have to imagine that situation when you're considering who to ask for a Gaelic tattoo translation.

Finally, even if your Gaelic-speaking friend is fluent and literate, be cautious. Even native speakers can make spelling or grammar mistakes and typos.

Real-life examples

Now that we have explored the various misguided ways that people attempt English-to-Gaelic translation, here are descriptions of some real-life examples of Gaelic tattoos with mistakes.

Military service

An ex-paratrooper wanted a Gaelic tattoo to commemorate his Scottish roots and a family tradition of airborne military service.

Figure 4 illustrates a similar concept. The design, combining the airborne parachute symbol and Gaelic words, was probably supposed to mean "family tradition." Unfortunately it does not.

The tattoo says "*AITHRIS A NA DREAM*." Perhaps someone thought that *aithris* meant "tradition" because "oral tradition" translates as *beul-aithris*. However, *aithris* actually means "report, account, recitation, or narration" (while *beul* means "mouth"). For example, *Aithris na Maidne* (Morning Report) is the BBC's Gaelic morning radio news program.

Dream can mean people, kindred, or folk, but it's not the usual Scottish Gaelic word for family, which is *teaghlach*. *À* means "out of" and so it's possible that this word was mistakenly used for "of," which is *de*.

Figure 4: *Aithris a na dream*, **an incorrect Gaelic tattoo design**

So, the way this tattoo reads to a Gaelic speaker is somewhat non-sensical: "report out of the people."

This grammatical construction—"family tradition" or "tradition of the family"—would require another grammatical change, however, because it uses something called the genitive case. The genitive case is a category that applies to nouns when used in expressions of possession, measure, or origin. In English we can use either "of" or a possessive apostrophe and "s" to indicate this relationship, for example "Mary's coat" or "the coat of Mary"; "a month's vacation," or "a month of vacation." But in Gaelic, the nouns themselves are modified in spelling and pronunciation when they are used in the genitive case. In the literal Gaelic translation of an English phrase like "family tradition," or "tradition of the family," the word for family (*teaghlach*) would be written in the genitive case, so it would read *dualchas teaghlaich*.

Even with these changes, however, *dualchas teaghlaich* sounds a bit odd because the second word is redundant. The Gaelic word *dualchas* alone conveys not only "tradition," but also the meaning of "family tradition." So after all, "*dualchas*" would have been the correct translation for the "family tradition" tattoo.

Honouring a family member

A young woman wanted a tattoo to honour her grandfather. In the similar design illustrated in Figure 5, the Celtic knotwork, Celtic lettering, and Gaelic combine to convey this message.

Unfortunately the words are incorrect because of a special feature in the Celtic languages called "initial consonant mutation" or "lenition." With this feature, depending on the place of a noun in a sentence, the way that you pronounce the first consonant of that noun can change.

The possessive *mo* (my) changes the initial consonant of the noun it modifies. In the Scottish Gaelic writing system, this sound change is usually indicated by placing an "h" after the initial consonant. *Mo + seanair = mo sheanair. Mo + gràdh = Mo ghràdh.* This changes the pronunciation of the word according to which sound is being lenited. In this case, *seanair* (pronounced something like "shen-er") becomes *sheanair* (pronounced "hen-er"). If the noun starts with

Figure 5: *Mo seanair, mo gaisgeach, mo gràdh,* an incorrect Gaelic tattoo design

a vowel, then it's just *m'* instead of *mo*. *Mo* + *anam* = *M' anam*. A grammar book tells you these kinds of rules, but you have to know how to look for and apply them.

So, with the lenition, this tattoo should read "*mo sheanair, mo ghaisgeach, mo ghràdh.*" But this still doesn't sound quite right. The first reason is that when referring to love for family members, the word *gaol* might be preferable to *gràdh*. *Gaol* developed historically from a word meaning "kin" or "kinship," while *gràdh* has always been used for romantic love as well as love of God. *Mo ghràdh*, when used as a term of endearment, is closer to "my darling" or "my sweetie pie."

You wouldn't normally refer to your grandfather as "my darling" in Gaelic; this sounds more like romantic love. One way to maintain some grammatical parallelism in the phrase (*mo* + 1, *mo* + 2, *mo* + 3) without the possible romantic weirdness would be to modify it thus: "*mo sheanair, mo ghaisgeach, mo ghaol ort,*" meaning "My grandfather, my hero, I love you" (literally, my love on you).

Keep in mind that there are two different ways of indicating possession in Gaelic. One is the *mo* ("my") construction which is similar to English. The other is nothing like English and involves prepositional pronouns. These are Gaelic words that combine both a preposition and a pronoun and they are a special challenge for most Gaelic learners.

For example, the preposition "at" is *aig* and the way to say "at me" is *agam*. At you, *agad*. At them, *aca*. And so on. These prepositional pronouns are used to express possession in Gaelic: for example, "my thing" is literally "the thing at-me"—*an rud agam*.

These two different ways of indicating possession are not totally interchangeable. In general, the first construction (*mo, do*) is used for things that are very close to you and/or cannot be given or taken away, including but not limited to your body parts, your children, and your clothing.

The second construction (at-me, at-you) is generally used to describe material possessions that people own. There are exceptions, however. For example, "my wife" is *mo bhean*, but "my husband" is *an duine agam*. *Mo nighean* can mean "my girl" in the sense of girlfriend, while *an nighean agam* can mean "my daughter"—but this is not a hard and fast rule, either (as the glossary shows).

Finally, having said all that, poetic license also allows some leeway in selecting the grammatical form of possession. In this case, keeping the parallelism by using *mo* for every part of the phrase is acceptable.

Scottish nationalist sentiment

A man in Scotland wanted a tattoo to express his Scottish nationalist sentiment and unfortunately received a design similar to the one illustrated in Figure 6.

This one was intended to say "Free Scotland." The biggest problem with the tattoo is that a Gaelic spelling mistake transformed the Gaelic *saor* into the English "soar"—an easy mistake to make when the English word is so close in spelling and neither the tattooer nor the tattooed knows Gaelic.

There are other problems with the spelling, but first we need to clarify whether *saor* was intended to be an adjective or a verb.

If *saor* is an adjective ("Free Scotland" means a Scotland that is free), the placement and spelling of the adjective must be changed. Gaelic is like French in regard to adjective placement—most of the adjectives come after the noun. And like French, Gaelic nouns are either masculine or feminine and adjectives change in spelling and pronunciation when they modify feminine nouns. *Saor* goes after the noun, and it modifies *Alba*, which is feminine, so "free Scotland" should be *Alba shaor*.

If *saor* is intended as an imperative verb, an order or appeal to free or liberate Scotland (as in "Free Nelson Mandela"), then it would be placed before the noun. But the second-person imperative in Gaelic comes in two versions, singular and plural (again like French with *tu* and *vous* forms). "*Saor Alba*" would still be in the singular—an order given to one person only, familiar or of equal or lower status.

Figure 6: *Soar Alba*, an incorrect Gaelic tattoo design

It might be better to use the second-person plural which gives a connotation of request or encouragement: "*Saoraibh Alba,*" "Liberate Scotland, all of you."

But perhaps the best choice would be to use the third-person imperative, "*Gun saoradh Alba*" which would translate as "Let Scotland Be Free" (in other words, "May Scotland Be Free").

"Free Scotland," whether adjective or verb, is a perfectly understandable nationalist sentiment. I suggest that the best way to honour Scotland's Celtic heritage and respect Gaelic as a language of Scotland is by taking care with the translation of Scottish nationalist sentiments from English into Gaelic.

Love for a partner

A woman wanted to express her love for her partner by getting a large script translation of "You are half of me" on her torso. An illustration of a similar style is in Figure 7.

The language of this tattoo is more subtly problematic than the previous examples. Literally it says "You Are Like Half Of-me" (with a missing accent mark over *dhìom* and non-standard capitalization). Idiomatically it does not sound right at all. In fact, it sounds English, even though it's in Gaelic.

Many fluent speakers have negative gut reactions to this kind of English-influenced Gaelic. One fluent speaker said it gave him a headache. Another said, "Yeah, well, it would at least be understood—it's typical English-speaker's *Gàidhlig* but it's so icky."

The problem is that a translation like this can't be fixed by correcting a word or two, because the entire sentence is out of keeping with idiomatic patterns of Gaelic.

The "*Tha thu*" is clunky and problematic, but I'll focus on "*leth dhìom*" which does literally translate as "half of-me" (*dhìom* is another one of those prepositional pronouns). The problem is that the word and idea of "half" are used somewhat differently in Gaelic than in English. You wouldn't normally leave *leth* dangling on its own when it's used to describe a portion of something—*leth-chuid* (half-portion) is the expression that's usually used for half of something.

Leth is used in other compound words for common half portions of things, like *leth-phinnt* for a half-pint of beer or milk. *Leth* is additionally used to form many other compounds in ways that are somewhat different from English. Examples include:

- *leth-shùil (one eye of two, lit. half-eye)*

- *leth-innis (peninsula, lit. half-island)*

- *leth-chù (mongrel, lit. half-dog)*

- *leth-asal (mule, lit. half-donkey)*

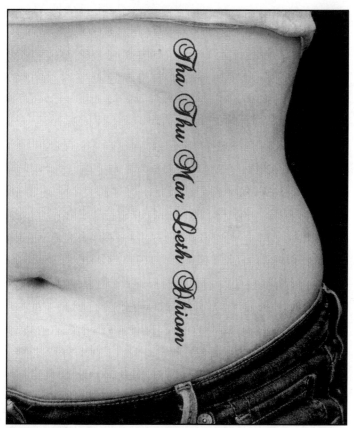

Figure 7: *Tha Thu Mar Leth Dhiom*, an incorrect Gaelic tattoo design

These examples illustrate the differences in the Gaelic cultural conceptions of "half" as expressed in the Gaelic language.

I asked one scholar who has studied centuries of Gaelic literature how she would translate the original English concept for this tattoo into Gaelic. She suggested adapting a line from an early 13th century poet about his wife's death. The line translates as "She was the very half of my soul." It uses a different compound word with *leth*, one that has fallen out of common use but still makes perfect sense today.

In modernized Scottish Gaelic the line would be *Bu cheart-leth m' anama i*. The original third-person past tense is suitable for memorials to a deceased loved one. Changed to the present tense, "She is the very half of my soul," it would be *'S ceart-leth m' anama i*. In the second person like the tattoo example above, "You are the very half of my soul" would be *'S tu ceart-leth m' anama*. (These are listed together with other variations in the glossary in Chapter 5.)

This poetic adaptation is an example of Gaelic idiom with authentic Gaelic flavour, as opposed to Gaelic with an English flavour. A metaphor can help explain the difference between the two. Say you put a plastic bag of cheese crackers in your bag or backpack, and it sits next to a pack of peppermint chewing gum for a few days. Then you get hungry one day while you're out of the house and remember the crackers. You take one out of the bag, bite into it… and it tastes like peppermint. The strong peppermint flavour has seeped through the gum wrapper, through the plastic bag, and into the crackers. What you're eating is still a cheese cracker—same orange colour, same crunch, same cheesy flavour. But now with tingly mint. Yuck. These flavours do not belong together.

Now, imagine that this Gaelic translation is the cheese cracker, and the English influence is the mint. Like mint, English is not inherently bad, but it doesn't really belong there. It flavours this example and many other Gaelic tattoos in a way that some Gaelic speakers would find just as repulsive as you might find a minty cheese cracker.

Gaelic tattoo ethics

At the end of the day, it's your tattoo and you can do anything you want with it. But when you ask for a Gaelic translation, you are involving someone else and their labour. You are also asking them to give of their culture for little or no reward. Just asking for one translation may seem like no big deal from your perspective, but when the requests from thousands of individuals are put together, they become a significant force.

The problem with tattoo requests is that Gaelic is not like English. It's an endangered minority language that multiple governments have tried for many hundreds of years to eliminate. Gaelic speakers have long been pressured to abandon the language and assimilate into the globalized, monolingual, English-speaking world; many did give it up. Given this long history, it's amazing that Gaelic language and culture still survive and thrive.

The "cool" factor comes from the rarity of Gaelic and positive but inaccurate stereotypes about Celtic languages and cultures. These stereotypes have little to do with how Gaelic speakers live their lives.

Free tattoo translation requests from English speakers are like death by a thousand paper cuts. They suck up the energy and goodwill of an endangered language community and usually give nothing back.

A proliferation of bad Gaelic tattoos also weakens the language. Every badly-translated tattoo that appears on the internet becomes an example for other people to follow. These bad examples propagate mistakes and makes the language more and more like a copy of English, and less and less like itself. Change happens to every language, but when the direction of change takes a language into convergence with a juggernaut like English, language death can result.

The following chapter suggests several ways to get an accurate Gaelic tattoo that supports the Gaelic language community and the future of the language.

Chapter 3

How to Choose a Gaelic Tattoo

The previous chapter described what can go wrong if you decide to get a Scottish Gaelic tattoo when you don't speak the language. Here are some positive suggestions for how to select a suitable Gaelic word or phrase for your tattoo. These are followed by a forewarning about the cultural implications of getting a Gaelic tattoo.

Use the glossary in this book

Chapter 5 contains a glossary of nearly 400 Scottish Gaelic words and phrases that are suitable for tattoos. The glossary includes multiple variations on popular concepts.

Several fluent Gaelic speakers in Scotland and in Nova Scotia have checked the translations in the glossary entries for spelling, grammar, sense, and aesthetics. All entries have been checked by at least three people, and some entries have undergone extensive discussion and multiple revisions.

Pay a professional translator

If you can't find what you're looking for in the glossary, find a professional Gaelic translator who will do the translation for you. This helps support the Gaelic language community in a concrete and meaningful way. If you are planning to spend a lot of money to have a design inked permanently onto your skin, then spend a bit more to ensure that it is correctly spelled and translated. You will have peace of mind, and your tattoo will be not only beautiful, but also meaningful and ethical.

Finding a professional translator who deals with Scottish Gaelic is not easy, because Gaelic is an endangered language. There are far fewer Gaelic translators in the world than translators of Mandarin Chinese, English, or Spanish.

Also, professional Gaelic translators may not want to take on your tattoo translation. They are busy translating longer texts for media, literature, business, and government needs.

Learn the language

The third suggestion requires a long-term commitment to the language. If Scottish Gaelic is so important that you want to inscribe it permanently on your skin, then it's not unreasonable to suggest that you spend a few years studying the language first, at your own pace, in whatever manner you can afford before getting a tattoo.

Studying the language will start to give you a feel for the culture and the kinds of things that people express in Gaelic. After several years, you still may not be fluent enough to make your own elaborate tattoo translation, but you will be able to do some simple ones. You may start to make friends and acquaintances with fluent speakers who would be willing to do a reliable translation out of goodwill, because you are involved with the language community.

Not knowing the language does not prevent you from tattooing it on your body, but if you take the time to get involved in Gaelic language and culture first, your tattoo will be even more deeply significant to you, and you will form rewarding relationships with other Gaelic speakers. This also ensures that your tattoo gives back to the language and its community and won't lead to accusations of cultural appropriation or any other kind of backlash.

Opportunities to learn the language include online classes, local classes in some communities, and even summer "destination" classes for people with the time and budget. I do not recommend using free websites like Memrise without also taking a class with a real teacher, whether in person or online.

Check the websites of these reputable Gaelic organizations for listings of face-to-face community classes in the U.S., Canada, Australia, New Zealand, and Scotland, and online classes that anyone can access with an internet connection:

- An Comunn Gàidhealach Ameireaganach, the American Scottish Gaelic Society: http://www.acgamerica.org/
- Comunn Gàidhlig Astràilia, the Scottish Gaelic Association of Australia: http://www.ozgaelic.org/
- CLÌ Gàidhlig: 21st Century Voice of Adult Gaelic Learners (Scotland): http://www.cli.org.uk/
- Sabhal Mòr Ostaig, the Gaelic college on the Isle of Skye (Scotland): http://www.smo.uhi.ac.uk/
- Ùlpan: Gaelic for Adults (Scotland): http://www.ulpan.co.uk/

Forewarning

Even if you plan a Gaelic tattoo carefully, not every fluent Gaelic speaker you meet will be thrilled to hear about it. There are several possible reasons for this.

First, right or wrong, some Gaelic speakers may still believe that tattoos carry a social stigma, just like some English speakers still do.

Second, some Gaels may find the idea of a Gaelic tattoo inauthentic because Gaelic-language tattoos are not a part of Gaelic culture. There is no archaeological or historical evidence of the Gaelic language ever being used in tattoos. Instead, such tattoos are an emerging multicultural and international trend, a product of contact between Gaelic- and English-speaking cultures.

Third, although every effort has been made to provide accurate and aesthetically pleasing Gaelic words and phrases in the glossary (see Chapter 5), in the end some of the entries are still translations from English, and represent ideas that fluent Gaelic speakers would not normally express in Gaelic. Additionally, speakers' dialect differences and educational backgrounds may impact what sounds acceptable to different Gaelic speakers.

Fourth, as discussed in Chapter 2, some native speakers cannot read and write Gaelic very well, or sometimes at all. A person who cannot spell Gaelic well may feel defensive if approached by someone who is interested in translating and writing the language for a tattoo, perhaps because they don't have the skills to help.

Finally, some Gaelic speakers see the language as belonging exclusively to them. Because the Gaelic language was dismissed, denigrated and attacked for so long in Scotland, many native Gaelic speakers came to accept the majority culture's negative view of their own language over the past several centuries. Some native speakers came to see the language not as a means of universal communication that could be learned and used by anyone, but rather as an in-group language that should properly belong only to them. Even some people who learned Gaelic as adults may feel that the only ones who have a right to learn and use the language are those who were born in a certain place; they may look down on or exclude others.

I do not believe in an overly possessive approach to the language, but I do believe that the best way to develop a feeling of connection to the language is to develop real-life connections to other people in a Gaelic language community. The language cannot survive in a social vacuum. Get involved in learning and speaking Gaelic with others, and help to support a language community by paying Gaelic speakers for Gaelic-related goods and services.

Now that you have some ideas about how to plan an ethical Gaelic tattoo, and the possible cultural implications of getting one, the following chapter will answer common questions about Gaelic writing, including the alphabet, spelling, and fonts.

Chapter 4

The Basics of Gaelic Writing

This chapter covers the most basic aspects of the Scottish Gaelic writing system, including the alphabet, spelling, accent marks and punctuation, fonts, and the pronunciation of the written word. These aspects of the language are vital to understand when planning a Gaelic tattoo.

The Gaelic alphabet

The Scottish Gaelic writing system uses the Latin or Roman alphabet, as English does. In fact, the Latin alphabet was used to write an earlier form of Gaelic before English even existed.

While the English alphabet consists of 26 letters, the Scottish Gaelic alphabet consists of 18 letters. The letters j, k, q, v, w, x, y, and z are not used. The Gaelic alphabet also contains accented vowels which include the grave-accented à, è, ì, ò, and ù. Texts printed in Nova Scotia, and pre-1981 printed texts from Scotland including coursebooks and dictionaries, also use the acute-accented á, é, and ó.

The Gaelic alphabet can be written in any Latin typeface or font, as long as the font includes the necessary accented characters; not all free and novelty fonts do. Even if your preferred font does not include accent marks, a tattoo artist can of course add the accents to the design where you indicate.

The phrase "Gaelic alphabet" is often used to refer to two other ideas. First, sometimes it refers to the Irish "Gaelic type" font; this font type style is covered in the section about fonts later in this chapter. Second, it can refer to the Gaelic tree alphabet, also called "*beith-luis-nuin*," which is a mnemonic device in Gaelic oral tradition where each letter of the alphabet is referred to by the archaic Gaelic name of a tree or plant that starts with that letter.

Gaelic spelling rules

Scottish Gaelic has formal spelling rules which have been modified from time to time. In the 6th century CE, the period after the Roman Empire, Old Irish was the first vernacular or native spoken language to be written with the Latin alphabet after the Latin of the Roman Empire itself. Old Irish is still studied by Celtic scholars and historical linguists today. This language, the ancestor language of modern Scottish Gaelic, was written before Old English, Old German, or Old French. This helps explain why Gaelic spelling conventions are so different from those familiar to us in English, German or French. The early Gaels created their own rules for how to represent the sounds of their language with Latin letters. The rules were changed over time as modern Scottish Gaelic eventually developed, but the Gaelic spelling and the sound system it represents remain quite different from English.

If you come to this system as a native speaker and reader of English, it appears to make no sense. However, Gaelic spelling rules are actually far more consistent than English rules.

Official Scottish Gaelic spelling rules have been modified twice in the past 35 years. What can make things a bit confusing is that not all Gaelic users have accepted all of these changes. Therefore, you may find that some words are spelled differently in different sources, depending on when and where they were published and whether the author or publisher followed the latest version of the spelling rules.

The strongest point of disagreement among Gaelic users is about the direction of accent marks over the vowels. A spelling reform committee decided in 1981 to eliminate the acute accent or *fada* (´) entirely, and only use the grave accent or *sràc* (`). The words previously written with acute-accented letters would henceforth be written with grave accents instead.

The 1981 spelling rules were imposed for secondary school exams in Scotland. Therefore, Scottish pupils, teachers, and other education professionals are required to follow them. Gaelic publishers in Scotland have also voluntarily adopted the changes. However, Gaelic teachers, writers, and publishers in Nova Scotia have not accepted them. A number of authors and academics in Scotland have chosen to ignore the revised spelling rules as well.

This book offers both the current Scottish spelling and, where different, the current Nova Scotian spelling, for every entry in the tattoo glossary.

Accent marks and apostrophes

All Gaelic teachers do agree about the importance of correctly using both accent marks and apostrophes. In Scottish Gaelic, accent marks are used above vowels to indicate a longer vowel length. Apostrophes are punctuation marks used in between words to indicate contractions. The functions of apostrophes and accent marks in Gaelic words are both essential and completely different from each other. Figure 8 on the following page illustrates the differences between apostrophes and accent marks in Scottish Gaelic.

Substituting an apostrophe for an accent mark is never correct in Gaelic. English speakers sometimes make this mistake in other languages. Occasionally you may see signs where the French word *café* is spelled with an apostrophe instead of an accent over the "e": *CAFE'*. Using an apostrophe in this way is incorrect. To avoid this kind of mistake with your tattoo design, copy the spelling of your desired word or phrase exactly from the glossary in Chapter 5, taking care with the direction of both accent marks and apostrophes. Double and triple check it.

Apostrophe

A punctuation mark used in between certain words to indicate contractions in Gaelic. For example:

cearcall a' chuain - circle of the ocean
m' eudail - my love (my treasure)

Accent Mark

A sign used above letters to indicate a different pronunciation, usually long vowels in Gaelic. For example:

ceòl na mara - music of the sea
le gràs Dhè - by the grace of God

Figure 8: Apostrophes vs. Accent Marks

You may see Gaelic writing on the internet which does not use the accent mark over a capital letter (for example, A or E instead of À or È). However, in Scottish Gaelic it is correct to use accented capital letters. Additionally, if your tattoo is entirely in capital letters (all caps) or in majuscule (fonts which do not have lower-case letters), then make sure to include the correct accent marks over the correct letters.

Which font to use

There are many beautiful free fonts available online that you can use to create the desired look for your Gaelic tattoo. Which font you pick depends on your tattoo artist's advice and your own design goals, including whether you prefer a contemporary or historical look. You don't need to use a "Celtic" style font for a Gaelic tattoo, but you certainly can if you wish.

One style associated strongly with Irish Gaelic is the *cló Gaelach* or "Gaelic type," a typeface which was based on handwritten Irish manuscript styles and used with movable type on Irish printing presses from the late 16th through mid-20th centuries. In the 1990s people started to design computer fonts based on Gaelic type designs. Today Gaelic type is mostly used for decorative purposes. Figure 9 illustrates a font used by the Irish government.

One special feature of Gaelic type is the dot which is used above a letter to represent lenition in Irish (for example, when a "b" sound becomes a "v" sound). Both Irish and Scottish Gaelic have lenition, but in the Latin script usually used for Scottish Gaelic, lenition is represented by an "h" following the letter.

Another special feature of Gaelic type is a sign called the Tironian "et" which is used in place of an ampersand (&). It looks similar to the numeral 7 and was originally developed in Latin and adopted by Irish monks. An example can be seen in the middle of the third line in Figure 9.

In general, people do not associate the Gaelic type style as closely with Scottish Gaelic as with Irish. Although handwritten Scottish Gaelic manuscripts used Gaelic or insular script styles, the first printed Scottish Gaelic book used Latin or Roman type. There was not a tradition of using movable Gaelic type to print books and periodicals in Scottish Gaelic as there was for Irish.

Scottish artist George Bain (1881–1968) revisited the common Irish and Scottish Gaelic manuscript and art tradition, using hand-drawn Gaelic type styles in his Celtic revival arts and crafts and the enduringly popular book *Celtic Art: The Methods of Construction*,

Cuaiġ bé móṁráċ le olúċrpáo ḟíonḟinn ṁí haṫa mo ḋea-ṗoṁcáin biṡ. jkquwxy ⁊ z Ⓠ 1234567890: Ouibhlinn an cló a úṡáiotear anseo.

Figure 9: The Duibhlinn digital font, designed in 1993, based on classic 1930s Gaelic type

first published in 1951. Nowadays some people choose to use Gaelic type fonts for Scottish Gaelic for a variety of reasons including aesthetic preference, a wish to evoke the common Gaelic heritage of Ireland and Scotland, or a desire to symbolize a personal connection with Ireland.

Other beautiful Celtic-style fonts are also available free for non-commercial use. My personal favourites from a design perspective are listed in Figure 10, including two different versions of the *cló Gaelach* or Gaelic type. Among the Gaelic type fonts, it appears that only Glanchló contains the full set of characters with lenition dots for writing Irish. Celtic Gaeilge has only the dotted d and h. The lenition dots are not needed for writing Scottish Gaelic, however.

If you want a look that is historically accurate yet not typically Celtic-looking, you could choose a font based on secretary hand, a common handwriting style in 16th and 17th-century Germany, England, Wales, and Scotland. It was a cursive style used to write vernacular Scottish Gaelic script in Scottish manuscripts including the Book of the Dean of Lismore (see the last line of Figure 10).

How to pronounce Gaelic

Once you've received your Gaelic tattoo, you may want to tell people about it. If it's in a visible location, people will probably start to notice it. They may ask you about it. How will you explain it if you can't pronounce it?

The pronunciation of Scottish Gaelic spelling is actually more regular and predictable than English—if you can speak and read Gaelic, that is. Every letter and combination of letters in Gaelic has its own corresponding sound. English speakers just aren't used to seeing the Latin alphabet used in such a different way. The letter combinations "bh" and "mh" are pronounced "v," "si" is pronounced "shee" and there are three different "l" sounds and three or four different "r" sounds.

If you're not a Gaelic speaker, several options are available to learn how to pronounce a word like *teaghlach* (family). First, some glossary words are found at learngaelic.net in the LearnGaelic online dictionary. Look up a word and click on the speaker icon to hear it.

Aon Cari

Aon Cari Celtic by Cari Buziak

Bunchló na Nod

Bunchló na Nod by Gaelchló

Celtic Gaeilge

Celtic Gaeilge by The Celtic Lady

Erin go Bragh

Erin go Bragh by Iconian Fonts

Glanchló

Glanchló by Vincent Morley

Irish Uncialfabeta

Irish Uncialfabeta by Manfred Klein

Kells SD

Kells SD by Steve Deffeyes

Secretary Hand Ancient

Secretary Hand Ancient

Figure 10: Some free fonts for Gaelic tattoos

Second, pronunciation videos for the glossary entries in this book will be released at gaelic.co/fuaimneachadh on the Gaelic Revitalization blog.

Finally, if you want more details about the exact placement of the lips, tongue, etc., the book *Blas na Gàidhlig* (The Flavour of Gaelic) by Michael Bauer explains in detail how to pronounce the sounds of the Scottish Gaelic language.

The basics of Gaelic writing are essential to an accurate Gaelic tattoo. Armed with this knowledge, you can make full use of the glossary in the next chapter, which provides nearly 400 suitable Gaelic words and phrases.

Chapter 5

Gaelic Tattoo Glossary

The entries in this glossary have been compiled from many different sources, including internet discussion forums, social media posts, e-mail requests, requests received by other Gaelic speakers, dictionaries, and songs. Please read on for guidance regarding how to search the glossary, the format of the entries, information on Gaelic grammar and capitalization, and background on the sources of the Bible verses and traditional proverbs.

How to use the glossary

The glossary contains nearly 400 different tattoo wording ideas, most of which originate in English and were translated into Scottish Gaelic, with the rest originating in Gaelic and an English translation provided.

The entries are divided into categories. Within each category, words and phrases are arranged somewhat alphabetically, but with thematic variations taking precedence.

Please keep in mind that not every glossary entry will be relevant or appealing to every reader. Tattoos are intensely personal and what one person finds beautiful, another may find offensive. Please disregard the sections or entries that do not express your own beliefs or values. The inclusion of an entry in the glossary does not imply that the author or publisher agrees with the idea or sentiment it expresses.

How to search

You can search the glossary in two ways. The first way is to browse through the various categories. For example, if you want a tattoo idea relating to a living family member, you can browse in the "Family" section.

The second way is to search in the glossary index at the back of the book. In the index, every English word and concept is listed alphabetically, followed by the unique number of the glossary entry or entries that contain that word or concept. A few words and concepts are used in entries listed in multiple sections. The index entry "Gaelic expressions" lists the most culturally Gaelic phrases and expressions.

Format of entries

Each entry follows the same format. First, the English word or phrase is given in **bold** type. In some cases this may be followed by information in *italics* which clarifies the part of speech, meaning, or usage. The abbreviations *lit.* (literally) or *adj.* (adjective) may be used.

The Gaelic translation follows in regular type. Some entries include two similar translations. In this case, the first one represents the current correct Gaelic spelling in Scotland. The second translation, marked with a single asterisk (*), represents the spelling which is current in Nova Scotia. Either spelling is suitable for use in a tattoo. (See Chapter 4 for more explanation about Gaelic spelling.)

In a few cases the second entry is marked with a double asterisk (**); these versions use an expression with a grammatical form which is technically correct but now seen as poetic and old-fashioned.

Parts of speech

Where necessary to avoid confusion, some single-word glossary entries are designated as a noun, adjective, or verb. These categories, known as "parts of speech," describe words by their function in a sentence. In English, sometimes the same word may represent several different parts of speech and meanings. For example, the word "free" is either an adjective or an imperative verb, depending on its context. However, in Gaelic, these different meanings are usually represented by different words.

Pay special attention to the parts of speech if you plan to combine different words into a single tattoo design that takes the form of a series of words, for example "family, love, life" or "friendship, love, loyalty." Make sure that all of the words are the same part of speech, for example, all nouns. Do not mix nouns, verbs, and adjectives.

Pronouns, which are parts of speech that can take the place of nouns, are also different in Gaelic. Gaelic is a language with two separate second-person pronouns, one for singular or informal "you" and another for plural or formal "you." Sociolinguists call this the T/V distinction (from Latin *tu* and *vos*, the precursor to French *tu* and *vous*) and it is found in many languages including French and Spanish, but not in modern English.

In T/V languages, verbs can take either a T or V form depending on which pronoun is used. A number of glossary entries are commands and appeals using imperative verbs. These verbs are designated as either "second-person singular or informal" or "second-person plural or formal." For some entries, you may select either the T or V version, according to whether you envision the command or appeal in your tattoo as being addressed to only yourself, or to a group of people, and whether you wish the language to sound more informal or formal.

Capitalization

All glossary entries are capitalized for the sake of uniformity, whether single words, phrases, or sentences. Proper nouns (names of persons and places) are also capitalized, following the rules of both Gaelic and English. The capitalization of a tattoo is up to you. One of the following three options is recommended: 1) upper-case for the first word and proper nouns only; 2) all lower-case letters; or 3) all upper-case (capitals). All lower-case or all upper-case is recommended for single words.

Bible verse excerpts

Several glossary sections contain phrases and excerpts from popular Christian Bible verses. These are drawn from the translation first published in 1801, incorporating a New Testament translation first published in 1767. The language of this translation is antiquated but it is still the most current version available. A new translation is being prepared by the Scottish Bible Society with translators from the Church of Scotland, Free Church of Scotland, and Roman Catholic Church, but it has not yet been published.

Gaelic proverbs

The final section lists some Gaelic proverbs. There are many more Gaelic proverbs in existence, but I only chose ones that seemed most desirable for English speakers to select as a tattoo. If Gaelic proverbs are a category you want to explore, then browse in the book *A Collection of Gaelic Proverbs and Familiar Phrases* edited by Alexander Nicolson, revised and reprinted by Birlinn.

The Gaelic Tattoo Glossary

Place and identity

1. **Birthplace** *(or heredity, or native or hereditary temper or "blood")*
   Dùthchas

2. **Heritage** *(or tradition)*
   Dualchas

3. **Homesickness** *(or sadness, nostalgia; related to exile from homeland)*
   Cianalas

4. **My beloved land**
   Tìr mo ghràidh

5. **Cape Breton**
   Ceap Breatainn

6. **Cape Breton girl**
   Nighean Cheap Breatainn

7. **Island girl**
   Nighean an eilein

8. **Cape Breton Island is the island that I love** *(title and line from the chorus of a well-known Gaelic song)*
   Eilean Cheap Breatainn 's e eilean mo rùin

9. **Cape Breton is the land of my love** *(the title of a well-known Gaelic song)*
   'S e Ceap Breatainn tìr mo ghràidh

10. **Land of trees and high mountains** *(second line from the chorus of the song in #9)*
    Tìr nan craobh 's nam beanntan àrd

11. **The most beautiful land on earth for us** *(fourth line from the chorus of the song in #9)*
Tìr as àillidh leinn air thalamh

12. **My heart is in Cape Breton**
Tha mo chridhe ann an Ceap Breatainn
Tha mo chridhe ann an Ceap Breatuinn*

13. **Cape Breton is where my heart is** *(with colloquial poetic usage, omitting extra 'ann' after 'S ann')*
'S ann an Ceap Breatainn far a bheil mo chridhe
'S ann an Ceap Breatuinn far a bheil mo chridhe*

14. **My heart is in Nova Scotia** *(third version with most old-fashioned poetic usage)*
Tha mo chridhe ann an Alba Nuadh
Tha mo chridhe ann an Albainn Nuaidh**
Tha mo chridhe an Albainn Nuaidh**

15. **Nova Scotia is where my heart is** *(with colloquial poetic usage, omitting extra 'ann' after 'S ann')*
'S ann an Alba Nuadh far a bheil mo chridhe
'S ann an Albainn Nuaidh far a bheil mo chridhe**

16. **Nova Scotia**
Alba Nuadh

17. **Pictou County**
Siorramachd Phictou

18. **Son of the Hector** *(descendant of Gaelic immigrants who came on the Ship Hector to Pictou, Nova Scotia, 1773)*
Mac an Eachainn
Mac an Eachuinn*

19. **Daughter of the Hector** *(descendant of Gaelic immigrants who came on the Ship Hector to Pictou, Nova Scotia, 1773)*
Nighean an Eachainn
Nighean an Eachuinn*

20. **Made in Cape Breton**
Dèante ann an Ceap Breatainn
Dèanta ann an Ceap Breatuinn*
Dèanta an Ceap Breatuinn** *(most poetic/old-fashioned)*

21. **Made in Nova Scotia**
Dèante ann an Alba Nuadh
Dèanta ann an Albainn Nuaidh**
Dèanta an Albainn Nuaidh** *(most poetic/old-fashioned)*

22. **Made in Canada**
Dèante ann an Canada
Dèanta ann an Canada*
Dèanta an Canada* *(most poetic/old-fashioned)*

23. **Farewell to Cape Breton**
Soraidh le Ceap Breatainn
Soraidh le Ceap Breatuinn*

24. **Farewell to Nova Scotia** *(the English title of a famous Nova Scotian folk song)*
Soraidh le Alba Nuadh
Soraidh le Albainn Nuaidh**

25. **Free Scotland** *("free" is an adjective that describes Scotland, i.e. a Scotland that is free)*
Alba shaor

26. **Free Scotland** *(plural or formal imperative verb; an order or appeal to "liberate Scotland")*
Saoraibh Alba

27. **Let Scotland be free** *(third-person imperative verb; "May Scotland be free")*
Gun saoradh Alba

28. **Freedom**
Saorsa
Saoirse*

29. **Freedom alone** *(from English translation of original Latin phrase in the Declaration of Arbroath, 1320: "For we fight not for glory, nor riches, nor honours, but for Freedom alone, which no good man gives up except with his life.")*
Gun ach saorsa
Gun ach saoirse*

30. **I am a Gael**
'S Gàidheal mi

31. **I am a Scot**
'S Albannach mi

32. **Made in Scotland**
Dèante ann an Alba
Dèanta ann an Albainn**

33. **My heart is in Scotland**
Tha mo chridhe ann an Alba
Tha mo chridhe ann an Albainn**

34. **My heart is in the Highlands** *(the English title of a famous Robert Burns poem/song)*
Tha mo chridhe air a' Ghàidhealtachd

35. **Scot** *(Scottish person, gender neutral)*
Albannach

36. **Scot** *(female Scottish person)*
Ban-Albannach

37. **Scotland**
Alba

38. **Scotland forever**
Alba gu bràth

39. **The clans of the Gael shoulder to shoulder** *(Gaelic expression)*
Clanna nan Gàidheal an guaillibh a chèile
Clanna nan Gàidheal an guaillibh a chéile*

40. **Wonderful Scotland** *(title of the Gaelic version of the song "Scotland the Brave"; a substitute, not a translation)*
Alba an Àigh

Family

41. **Blood makes you related; loyalty makes you family**
'S e fuil an dàimh ach dìleas an càirdeas

42. **Family**
Teaghlach

43. **Family tradition**
Dualchas

44. **Family first**
Teaghlach an toiseach

45. **Family forever**
Teaghlach gu bràth

46. **Family is an unbreakable bond** *(lit. family cannot be broken)*
Cha ghabh teaghlach sgaradh

47. **Family is everything** *(lit. family is the most important)*
'S e an teaghlach as cudromaiche
'S e an teaghlach as cudthromaiche*

48. **Family is life** *(lit. no life without family)*
Chan eil beatha ann gun teaghlach

49. **Family, faith, forgiveness**
Teaghlach, creideamh, maitheanas

50. **Family, clan and country**
Teaghlach, cinneadh agus dùthaich

51. **My family, my blood, my life**
Mo theaghlach, mo dhùthchas, mo bheatha

52. **Honour thy father and mother** (*Bible, Exodus 20:12, first half of the verse*)
Thoir urram dod athair is dod mhàthair
Thoir urram do d' athair agus do do mhàthair*

53. **Honour your family, clan, and country**
Thoir urram dod theaghlach, chinneadh agus dhùthaich
Thoir urram do d' theaghlach, chinneadh agus dhùthaich*

54. **Live for yourself, die for your family**
Bi beò air do sgàth-sa, gabh bàs air sgàth 's an teaghlaich

55. **Mother**
Màthair

56. **Mom** (*or Mum*)
Mamaidh

57. **Mommy** (*or Mummy*)
Mamaidh

58. **My mother**
Mo mhàthair

59. **My beloved mother**
Màthair mo ghràidh

60. **Beloved mother**
Màthair mo ghràidh

61. **Honour your mother**
Thoir urram dod mhàthair
Thoir urram do d' mhàthair*

62. **Father**
Athair

63. **My father**
M' athair

64. **Beloved father**
Athair mo ghràidh

65. **My beloved father**
Athair mo ghràidh

66. **My mother and father**
Mo mhàthair is m' athair

67. **Dad**
Dadaidh

68. **Daddy**
Dadaidh

69. **Honour thy father**
Thoir urram dod athair
Thoir urram do d' athair*

70. **Like father, like son** *(Gaelic expression)*
Gille athar

71. **Follow close the fame of your fathers** *(Gaelic expression)*
Lean gu dlùth ri cliù do shinnsrean

72. **Grandfather**
Seanair

73. **My grandfather**
Mo sheanair

74. **Beloved grandfather**
Seanair mo ghràidh

75. **My beloved grandfather**
Seanair mo ghràidh

76. **My grandfather, my hero, I love you** *(lit. my love on you)*
Mo sheanair, mo ghaisgeach, mo ghaol ort

77. **Grandmother**
Seanmhair

78. **My grandmother**
Mo sheanmhair

79. **Beloved grandmother**
Seanmhair mo ghràidh

80. **My beloved grandmother**
Seanmhair mo ghràidh

81. **Grandchild**
Ogha

82. **Grandchildren**
Oghaichean

83. **Cousin** *(first cousin)*
Co-ogha

84. **Cousins** *(first cousins)*
Co-oghaichean

85. **Sister**
Piuthar

86. **Sisters**
Peathraichean

87. **My sister**
Mo phiuthar

88. **Beloved sister**
Piuthar mo ghràidh

89. **My beloved sister**
Piuthar mo ghràidh

90. **Beautiful sisters**
Peathraichean bòidheach

91. **Oldest sister** *(eldest)*
Piuthar as sine

92. **Middle sister**
Piuthar sa mheadhan
Piuthar 'sa mheadhan*

93. **Youngest sister** *(littlest)*
Piuthar as òige

94. **My sister, my friend**
Mo phiuthar, mo charaid

95. **Sisters forever**
Peathraichean gu bràth

96. **Sisters by chance, friends by choice**
Peathraichean air thuairmeas, caraidean air roghainn

97. **My sister, my best friend, my rock** *(literal translation)*
Mo phiuthar, mo charaid, mo charraig

98. **Brother**
Bràthair

99. **Brothers**
Bràithrean

100. **Beloved brother**
Bràthair mo ghràidh

101. **My brother**
Mo bhràthair

102. **My beloved brother**
Bràthair mo ghràidh

103. **Baby** (*only in the sense of infant*)
Leanabh

104. **My baby** (*infant only*)
Mo leanabh

105. **My babies** (*infant only*)
Mo leanabhan

106. **My children are my world**
Mo chlann mo shaoghal

107. **Children**
Clann

108. **Daughter**
Nighean

109. **My daughter**
Mo nighean

110. **My beautiful daughter**
Mo nighean àlainn

111. **My girls are my world**
Mo chlann-nighean mo shaoghal

112. **My girls**
Mo chlann-nighean

113. **Two beautiful daughters**
Dithis nighean àlainn

114. **Three beautiful daughters**
Triùir nighean àlainn

115. **Four beautiful daughters**
Ceathrar nighean àlainn

116. **Five beautiful daughters**
Còignear nighean àlainn
Cóignear nighean àlainn*

117. **Son**
Mac

118. **My son**
Mo mhac

119. **My boys**
Mo ghillean

120. **Two handsome boys**
Dithis ghillean grinne

121. **Three handsome boys**
Triùir ghillean grinne

122. **Four handsome boys**
Ceathrar ghillean grinne

123. **Five handsome boys**
Còignear ghillean grinne
Cóignear ghillean grinne*

124. **Two beautiful girls and one handsome boy**
Dithis nighean àlainn is gille grinn

125. **One beautiful girl and two handsome boys**
Nighean àlainn is dithis ghillean grinne

126. **A son like his mother, and a daughter like her father**
(Gaelic expression)
Mac mar a mhàthair, 's nighean mar a h-athair

Love and friendship

127. **Eternal love**
Gaol gu bràth

128. **Eternally**
Gu sìorraidh

129. **Eternally and forever**
Gu suthainn 's gu sìorraidh
Gu suthainn 's gu sìorruidh*

130. **Everlasting**
Bith-bhuan

131. **Faith, love, hope, happiness**
Creideamh, gràdh, dòchas, sonas

132. **For my love**
Son mo ghaoil
'Son mo ghaoil*

133. **Forever** *(lit. until the ocean becomes the beach; Gaelic expression)*
Gun tèid an cuan na tràigh
Gun téid an cuan 'na tràigh*

134. **Forever** *(for eternity; lit. until Doomsday/Judgement Day)*
Gu bràth

135. **Forever** *(lit. to the end)*
Gu deò

136. **Forever and a day** *(lit. the day after Doomsday)*
Là an dèidh Là Luain

137. **Forever and ever**
Gu sìorraidh buan
Gu sìorruidh buan*

138. **Forever and ever**
Gu suthain sìorraidh
Gu suthain sìorruidh*

139. **Friend**
Caraid

140. **Best friend**
Caraid as teinne

141. **Friendship**
Càirdeas

142. **Friendship and kindness**
Càirdeas is coibhneas
Càirdeas is caoimhneas*

143. **Husband**
Fear-chèile
Fear-chéile*

144. **Wife**
Bean-chèile
Bean-chéile*

145. **Husband and wife**
Fear is bean

146. **I am loved**
Is gràdhaichte mi

147. **I am my beloved's and my beloved is mine** (*Bible, Song of Solomon 6:3; "I" is female and "my beloved" is male in the original; "I" is gender neutral in this wording and "my beloved" is male in this wording*)
Is le fear mo ghràidh mise, agus is leamsa fear mo ghràidh.

148. **I am my beloved's and my beloved is mine** (*Bible, adapted from Song of Solomon 6:3; "I" is gender neutral and "my beloved" is female in this wording*)
Is le tè mo ghràidh mise, agus is leamsa tè mo ghràidh
Is le té mo ghràidh mise, agus is leamsa té mo ghràidh*

149. **I love you** (*lit. love is at me on you*)
Tha gaol agam ort

150. **I love you** (*lit. my love is on you*)
Tha mo ghaol ort

151. **Love**
Gràdh (*romantic or religious; also family*)
Gaol (*for family; also romantic*)

152. **Love is enough** (*lit. love will suffice*)
Foghnaidh gaol

153. **Love is patient, love is kind** (*Bible, from I Corinthians 13:4*)
Tha an gràdh fad-fhulangach agus coibhneal

154. **Love you always** (*lit. my love will be on you forever*)
Bidh mo ghaol ort gu bràth

155. **Loved** (*adj.*)
Gràdhaichte

156. **Lover**
Gràdhaiche (*someone who is loved; non-traditional*)
Gràdhadair (*someone who loves; non-traditional*)

157. **Loyalty, friendship, love** *(note accent over the "i" in dìlse)*
Dìlse, càirdeas, gràdh

158. **My brown-haired lass** *(or girl; Gaelic expression)*
Mo nighean donn

159. **My beautiful brown-haired lass** *(Gaelic expression)*
Mo nighean donn bhòidheach

160. **My beloved** *(beloved is male)*
Fear mo chridhe

161. **My beloved** *(beloved is female)*
Tè mo chridhe
Té mo chridhe*

162. **My eternal love** *(gender neutral)*
Mo rùn gu bràth

163. **My husband** *(lit. my male partner)*
M' fhear-chèile
M' fhear-chéile*

164. **My wife** *(lit. my female partner)*
Mo bhean-chèile
Mo bhean-chéile*

165. **My husband** *(lit. the man at-me)*
An duine agam

166. **My wife**
Mo bhean

167. **My love**
Mo ghaol

168. **My love** *(my darling, my sweetie)*
Mo ghràdh

169. **My love** (*lit. my secret*)
Mo rùn

170. **My love** (*lit. my treasure*)
M' eudail

171. **One flesh** (*Bible, from Mark 10:8*)
Aon fheòil

172. **Only you in my heart**
Gun ach thusa nam chridhe
Gun ach thusa 'nam chridhe*

173. **Partner** (*spouse or significant other; gender neutral*)
Cèile
Céile*
Càraid (*lit. a couple or pair. Accent over the "a"
differentiates it from "caraid" which has different
meaning*)

174. **My partner** (*spouse or significant other; gender neutral*)
Mo chèile
Mo chéile*
Mo chàraid (*see #173*)

175. **Sweetheart** (*or lover, or boyfriend/girlfriend; gender
neutral*)
Leannan

176. **My sweetheart** (*see #175*)
Mo leannan

177. **We are one flesh** (*Bible, from Mark 10:8*)
Tha sinn nar n-aon fheòil
Tha sinn 'nar n-aon fheòil*

178. **You are the very half of my soul**
'S tu ceart-leth m' anama

179. **He is the very half of my soul**
'S ceart-leth m' anama e

180. **She is the very half of my soul**
'S ceart-leth m' anama i

In memoriam

181. **Always** *(present tense, continual action or state)*
An-còmhnaidh
An còmhnuidh*

182. **Always** *(present tense, continual action or state,*
continually or at all times)
Daonnan

183. **Always in my heart**
Daonnan nam chridhe
Daonnan 'nam chridhe*

184. **Forever in my heart**
Nam chridhe gu bràth
'Nam chridhe gu bràth*

185. **Broken hearted**
Cridhe briste

186. **Everything that lives will die**
Thig gach nì beò gu bàs

187. **Until we meet again may God hold you in the palm
of his hand**
Gus tig sinn còmhla a-rithist, nach glèidh Dia thu na
làimh
Gus tig sinn còmhla a rithist, nach gléidh Dia thu 'na
làimh*

188. **Grief** *(or sorrow)*
Bròn

189. **He was the very half of my soul**
Bu cheart-leth m' anama e

190. **She was the very half of my soul**
Bu cheart-leth m' anama i

191. **Honour her memory** *(lit. a stone on her cairn; Gaelic expression)*
Clach air a càrn

192. **Honour his memory** *(lit. a stone on his cairn; Gaelic expression)*
Clach air a chàrn

193. **Honour our ancestors**
Urram dar sinnsearan
Urram d' ar sinnsearan*

194. **Honour them** *(lit. a stone on their cairn)*
Clach air an càrn

195. **In loving memory**
Mar chuimhneachan

196. **In memoriam**
Mar chuimhneachan

197. **In my heart**
Nam chridhe
'Nam chridhe*

198. **In my heart forever**
Nam chridhe gu bràth
'Nam chridhe gu bràth*

199. **Life and death**
Beatha is bàs

200. **My heart is heavy but my soul is strong**
'S trom mo chridhe ach 's treun m' anam

201. **May her soul rest in eternal peace**
Fois shìorraidh air a h-anam
Fois shìorruidh air a h-anam*

202. **May his soul rest in eternal peace**
Fois shìorraidh air anam
Fois shìorruidh air a dh'anam*

203. **May he have peace**
Fois gun d' fhuair e

204. **May she have peace**
Fois gun d' fhuair i

205. **Rest in peace** *(lit. eternal rest on **her** soul)*
Fois shìorraidh air a h-anam
Fois shìorruidh air a h-anam*

206. **Rest in peace** *(lit. eternal rest on **his** soul)*
Fois shìorraidh air anam
Fois shìorruidh air a dh'anam*

207. **Still living in the hearts left behind**
Beò fhathast an cridhean na fàgte

208. **Still living in the hearts you left behind**
Beò fhathast an cridhean a dh'fhàg thu

209. **Until I see you again**
Gus faic mi a-rithist thu
Gus faic mi a rithist thu*

210. **Until we meet again**
Gus an ath chèilidh
Gus an ath chéilidh*

211. **Without you, my love**
Às d' aonais, a ghràidh

Religious and spiritual

212. **Angel**
Aingeal

213. **Angels and demons**
Ainglean is deamhain

214. **In the arms of the angel**
An uchd an aingil

215. **Be still and know that I am God** *(Bible, from Psalms 46:10)*
Bithibh sàmhach, agus tuigibh gur mise Dia

216. **Be still** *(Bible, adapted from Psalms 46:10; familiar addressed to one person)*
Bi sàmhach

217. **Blessed**
Beannaichte

218. **Blessing**
Beannachd

219. **By grace** *(Bible; from Ephesians 2:8, "Oir is ann le gràs a tha sibh air 'ur tèarnadh…")*
Le gràs

220. **By the grace of God**
Le gràs Dhè
Le gràs Dhé*

221. **Demon**
Deamhan

222. **Druid**
Draoidh

223. **Everlasting life**
Beatha shìorraidh

224. **Evil**
Olc

225. **Faith, hope, and love** *(Bible, from I Corinthians 13:13)*
Creideamh, dòchas, agus gràdh

226. **Flame of God**
Lasair Dhè
Lasair Dhé*

227. **God**
Dia

228. **Goddess**
Ban-dia

229. **Good and evil**
Maitheas agus olc

230. **Goodness**
Maitheas

231. **Grace**
Gràs

232. **Grace of God**
Gràs Dhè
Gràs Dhé*

233. **Heaven**
Nèamh

234. **Hell**
Ifrinn

235. **Holy** *(adj.)*
Naomh

236. **Holy Spirit**
Spiorad Naomh

237. **Jesus** *(note accent mark over "I")*
Ìosa

238. **Jesus Christ** *(note accent mark over "I")*
Ìosa Crìost
Ìosa Crìosd*
Ìosa Crìosda** *(used in the Catholic prayer book* Iùl a'
Chrìosdaidh*)*

239. **Lord, make me an instrument of your peace.** *(First
line of the prayer of St. Francis of Assisi in hymn form;
Catholic Church translation)*
A Thighearna, dèan mise nam theachdaire sìth.
A Thighearna, dèan mise 'nam theachdaire sìth.*

240. **Magic**
Draoidheachd

241. **Mary** *(mother of Jesus)*
Moire

242. **Only God**
Dia a mhàin

243. **Pagan** *(adj. or noun)*
Pàganach

244. **Paradise**
Pàrras

245. **Pray for us**
Guidh air ar son

246. **Sacred** *(adj.)*
Naomh

247. **Sacred fire**
Teine naomh

248. **Sacred flame**
Lasair naomh

249. **Saint**
Naomh

250. **Sanctuary** *(or magic circle of protection)*
Caim

251. **Saved** *(Bible; adapted from Ephesians 2:8, "Oir is ann le gràs a tha sibh air 'ur tèarnadh...")*
Teàrnaichte

252. **Sinner**
Peacach

253. **So mote it be** *(So may it be; archaic)*
Guma h-amhlaidh

254. **The Devil**
An Diabhal

255. **The Father, the Son, and the Holy Spirit**
An t-Athair, am Mac, agus an Spiorad Naomh

256. **The Goddess**
A' Bhan-dia

257. **The Lord is my shepherd; I shall not want** *(Bible, Psalms 23:1)*
Is e an Tighearna mo bhuachaille; cha bhi mi ann an dìth

258. **The truth against the world**
An fhìrinn an aghaidh an t-saoghail

259. **Trinity**
Trianaid

260. **Watch over me** *(verb, second-person singular or familiar)*
Dèan m' fhaire

261. **Witch** *(female)*
Bana-bhuidseach

Courage, honour, and military service

262. **Conqueror**
Ceannsaiche

263. **Conquest**
Ceannsachadh

264. **Death before dishonour**
Bàs ro eas-onair

265. **Death from above** *(Airborne motto)*
Bàs às an uarach

266. **Defender**
Dìonadair

267. **Female fighter** *(or female champion; undaunted female)*
Muireardach

268. **Female warrior**
Bana-ghaisgeach

269. **Heroine**
Bana-ghaisgeach

270. **Fighter** *(gender neutral)*
Strìtheadair

271. **Follow me** *(U.S. Army Infantry motto)*
Lean mi *(verb, imperative singular or familiar)*
Leanaibh mi *(verb, imperative plural or formal)*

272. **Hero**
Gaisgeach

273. **Honour**
Onair

274. **Iron man**
Fear iarainn

275. **Keep the peace**
Ceangail sìth

276. **Mercy**
Tròcair

277. **My hero**
Mo ghaisgeach

278. **My soldier**
Mo shaighdear

279. **No fear** *(lit. without fear)*
Gun eagal

280. **No mercy** *(lit. without mercy)*
Gun tròcair

281. **Our hero**
Ar gaisgeach

282. **Our soldier**
Ar saighdear

283. **Patriot** *(lit. country-lover)*
Tìr-ghràdhaiche

284. **Protect and serve**
Dìon is cuidich

285. **Protector**
Dìonadair

286. **Second to none**
Barraichte

287. **Soldier**
Saighdear

288. **Soldier** *(or champion, hero)*
Laoch

289. **Vengeance**
Dìoghaltas

290. **Victory**
Buaidh

291. **Warrior** *(or hero, champion)*
Laoch

Work, activities, and identities

292. **Artist**
Dealbhadair *(lit. one who draws)*
Ealanaiche *(general sense of "the arts")*

293. **Atheist**
Eas-creidmheach *(lit. unbeliever)*
Neo-dhiadhaire *(lit. non-theist)*

294. **Athlete**
Lùth-chleasaiche

295. **Book-lover**
Sàr-leughadair

296. **Dance**
Dannsa

297. **Dancer**
Dannsair

298. **Doctor**
Dotair

299. **Fiddler**
Fìdhlear

300. **Firefighter**
Smàladair *(non-traditional word)*
Tè-smàlaidh *or* té-smalaidh* *(female)*
Fear-smàlaidh *(fireman, male)*
Neach-smàlaidh *(gender neutral)*

301. **Fisherman**
Iasgair

302. **Gambler**
Cearraiche

303. **Harper** *(or harpist)*
Clàrsair

304. **Healer** *(or physician)*
Lighiche

305. **Hunter**
Sealgair

306. **Mermaid**
Maighdeann-mhara

307. **Music**
Ceòl

308. **Musician**
Ceòladair *(non-traditional)*
Neach-ciùil *(lit. music-person)*

309. **Nurse**
Nurs *(contemporary word)*
Banaltram *(female; traditional word)*
Banaltruim*
Fear-altram *(male; non-traditional new word)*
Fear-altruim*
Neach-altram *(gender neutral; non-traditional new word)*
Neach-altruim*

310. **Performer** *(including actor, clown, juggler, comedian)*
Cleasaiche

311. **Piper** *(bagpiper)*
Pìobair

312. **Immigrant**
Eilthireach

313. **Pilgrim** *(or traveler)*
Taistealach

314. **Pirate**
Spùinneadair

315. **Poet**
Bàrd
Filidh

316. **Sailor**
Seòladair

317. **Stranger** *(or foreigner)*
Coigreach

318. **Teacher**
Tidsear *(most common word, gender neutral)*
Bana-theagaisg *(female)*
Fear-teagaisg *(male)*
Neach-teagaisg *(gender neutral)*

319. **Vegetarian**
Glasraichear *(lit. vegetable person)*
Feòil-sheachnair *(lit. one who gave up meat)*

Emotions, qualities, and concepts

320. **Alive** *(adj.)*
Beò

321. **Awake** *(adj., lit. wide awake)*
Làn fhaireachadh

322. **Beautiful** *(adj.)*
Bòidheach

323. **Beautiful fighter** *(female)*
Bana-ghaisgeach bhòidheach

324. **Beautiful warrior** *(gender neutral)*
Laoch eireachdail

325. **Bless you** *(singular or familiar "you"; lit. a blessing on you)*
Beannachd ort

326. **Breath** *(noun; can also mean air, vital spark, ray of light)*
Deò

327. **Breathe** *(second-person singular or familiar imperative verb)*
Gabh d' anail

328. **Confidence** *(or courage; noun)*
Misneachd

329. **Dream** *(noun)*
Bruadar
Aisling *(may also refer to old Irish political poetry which personifies Ireland as a woman)*

330. **Drug-free** *(adj.)*
Gun drug sam bith *(lit. without any drugs)*
A' seachnadh drugaichean *(lit. avoiding or abstaining from drugs)*

331. **Enough** *(noun)*
Gu leòr

332. **Plenty** *(noun)*
Pàilteas

333. **Faithful** *(adj.)*
Dìleas

334. **Fool** *(noun)*
Amadan *(male)*
Òinseach *(female)*

335. **Foolish** *(adj.)*
Gòrach

336. **Free** *(adj.)*
Saor

337. **Good fortune** *(or good luck, prosperity, success, or improvement)*
Piseach

338. **Good luck to you** *(singular or familiar "you"; lit. good luck on you)*
Piseach ort

339. **Good luck to you** *(singular or familiar "you"; lit. that well it goes with you)*
Gur math thèid leat
Gur math théid leat*

340. **Happiness** *(noun)*
Sonas

341. **Hate** *(noun)*
Gràin

342. **Healing** *(noun)*
Slànadh

343. **Hope** *(noun)*
Dòchas

344. **Infinity** *(or endlessness; noun)*
Neo-chrìochnachd

345. **Joy** *(noun)*
Aoibhneas

346. **Laughter** *(noun)*
Gàire

347. **Legacy** *(noun)*
Dìleab

348. **Life** *(noun)*
Beatha

349. **Life, laughter, love** *(nouns)*
Beatha, gàire, gaol

350. **Little by little**
Beag air bheag

351. **Love and hate** *(nouns)*
Gaol is gràin

352. **Mighty** *(adj.)*
Treun

353. **No regrets** *(lit. without regret)*
Gun duilichinn

354. **Peace** *(noun)*
Sìth

355. **Powerful** *(or mighty; adj.)*
Cumhachdach

356. **Pride** *(noun; could be given queer/LGBT connotation depending on context)*
Pròis

357. **Take a break** *(or take a rest; verb, second-person imperative, singular or familiar)*
Gabh fois

358. **Strong** *(adj.)*
Làidir

359. **Sacrifice** *(noun; note accent over the "i")*
Ìobairt

360. **Strength** *(noun)*
Neart

361. **Strong** *(adj.)*
Làidir

362. **Strong** *(adj.)*
Lùthmhor *(in the sense of strong or agile)*
Neartmhor *(in the sense of strong, powerful, or able)*

363. **Success and luck** *(nouns)*
Buaidh is piseach

364. **Unafraid** *(adj., lit. without fear)*
Gun eagal

Gaelic proverbs and expressions

365. **A house without a dog, a cat or a small child is a house without cheerfulness or laughter.**
Taigh gun chù, gun chat, gun leanabh beag, taigh gun ghean gun ghàire.

366. **A land without a tongue, a land without a soul**
("a tongue" in the sense of "a language")
Tìr gun teanga, tìr gun anam

367. **A little hole will sink a big ship.**
Bàthaidh toll beag long mhòr.
Bàthaidh toll beag long mhór.*

368. **A wave will rise on quiet water.**
Èiridh tonn air uisge balbh.
Éiridh tonn air uisge balbh.*

369. **After war comes peace.**
An dèidh cogaidh thig sìth.
An déidh cogaidh thig sìth.*

370. **As you value yourself, others will esteem you.**
A rèir do mheas ort fhèin, measaidh càch thu.
A réir do mheas ort fhéin, measaidh càch thu.*

371. **Better to rise [get up] late than not at all.**
'S fhearr èirigh anmoch na bhith gun èirigh idir.
'S fhearr éirigh anmoch na bhith gun éirigh idir.*

372. **Change is refreshing.**
Is ùrachadh atharrachadh.

373. **Do not surrender while you are alive.**
Na gèill is tu beò.
Na géill is tu beò.*

374. **Draw me not without cause, nor return me without honour** (*inscription for a sword; "pill" is the original archaic verb for "return" in this proverb; "till" is modernized*)
Na tarraing mi gun adhbhar, 's na till mi gun chliù
Na tarraing mi gun adhbhar, 's na pill mi gun chliù**

375. **He that conquers himself conquers an enemy.**
Am fear a thug buaidh air fhèin, thug buaidh air nàmhaid.
Am fear a thug buaidh air fhéin, thug buaidh air nàmhaid.*

376. **He who dares, wins.** (*lit. the man who dares not, wins not*)
Am fear nach misnich, cha bhuannaich.

377. **She who dares, wins.** (*feminized version of #376, non-traditional*)
An tè nach misnich, cha bhuannaich.
An té nach misnich, cha bhuannaich.*

378. **Let me eat, let me drink, let me sleep.**
Itheam, òlam, caidileam.

379. **Many a thing is golden that is not gold.**
Is iomadh rud buidhe nach òr.

380. **My own property, my own wife and 'Come home,' three of the sweetest words.**
Mo chuid fhèin, mo bhean fhèin is 'Tiugainn dachaigh,' trì faclan as blaisde th' ann.
Mo chuid fhéin, mo bhean fhéin is 'Tiugainn dachaigh,' trì faclan as blaisde th' ann.*

381. **No door ever shut but another opened.**
Cha do dhùin doras nach do fhosgail doras.

382. **Nothing can get into a closed fist.**
Cha tèid nì sam bith san dòrn dùinte.
Cha téid nì sam bith 'san dòrn dùinte.*

383. **Remember those you came from.**
Cuimhnich air na daoine bhon tàinig thu.
Cuimhnich air na daoine bho'n tàinig thu.*

384. **Think of the fortitude of your forefathers.**
Cuimhnich air cruadal nan daoine bhon tàinig thu.
Cuimhnich air cruadal nan daoine bho'n tàinig thu.*

385. **Sweet is a bird's voice where he was born.**
Is binn guth an eòin far am beirear e.

386. **Say little and say it well.**
Abair ach beagan is abair gu math e.

387. **The beginning of understanding is doubt.**
Tùs tuigse teagamh.

388. **The essence of a game is at its end.**
Brìgh gach cluiche gu dheireadh.

389. **The eyes of a friend are a good mirror.**
Is math an sgàthan sùil caraide.

390. **The man that knows is powerful.**
Is treun fear an eòlais.

391. **The woman that knows is powerful.** *(feminized version of #390, non-traditional)*
Is treun tè an eòlais.
Is treun té an eòlais.*

392. **The truth is better than gold.**
'S fheàrr an fhìrinn na 'n t-òr.

393. **There is no hero without a wound.**
Chan eil saoidh air nach laigh leòn.

394. **There is no rock that the stream won't change.**
Chan eil carraig air nach caochail sruth.

395. **There's a cure for every condition but death.**
Tha leigheas air gach càs, ach chan eil leigheas air a' bhàs.

396. **To each his own.**
A chàil fhèin aig a h-uile fear.
A chàil fhéin aig a h-uile fear.*

References

Introduction

Bad Hebrew Tattoos: Hebrew Translation and Spelling Mistakes (n.d.) URL: http://bad-hebrew-tattoos.blogspot.ca/

Hall, Ellie and Kevin Tang. (2013) "34 Ridiculous Chinese Character Tattoos Translated." Buzzfeed, 2 August. URL: http://www.buzzfeed.com/el-lievhall/ridiculous-chinese-character-tattoos-translated

Molloy, Mark (2015) "This man's Hebrew tattoo doesn't say what he thinks it does." *The Telegraph*, 14 May. URL: http://www.telegraph.co.uk/news/worldnews/northamerica/usa/11604906/This-mans-Hebrew-tattoo-doesnt-say-what-he-thinks-it-does.html

Chapter 1

Scotland's Census (n.d.) National Records of Scotland. URL: http://www.scotlandscensus.gov.uk/ods-web/standard-outputs.html (2011 Scottish census results).

Figure 1, information on Celtic languages adapted from Ethnologue: Languages of the World (n.d.) "Celtic." URL: http://www.ethnologue.com/sub-groups/celtic-0

Figure 2, Irish examples adapted from Nickel, Audrey (2012). "Irish Gaelic Greetings," Bitesize Irish Gaelic, 20 April. URL: http://www.bitesize.irish/blog/irish-gaelic-greetings/

Chapter 2

Bauer, Michael (n.d.). "Possessives and syllabic structure or Ar n-Athair a tha air nèamh," http://www.akerbeltz.org/index.php?title=Possessives_and_syllabic_structure_or_Ar_n-Athair_a_tha_air_n%C3%A8amh

Bauer, Michael (2015). "The spectre of Google Translate for Gaelic," https://akerbeltzalba.wordpress.com/2015/01/15/the-spectre-of-google-translate-for-gaelic/

Figure 4, Deutsche Uncialis font by Dieter Stegmann, free for commercial use (http://www.1001fonts.com/deutsche-uncialis-font.html)

Figure 5, Triquetra knot illustration, public domain image on Wikimedia Commons (https://commons.wikimedia.org/wiki/File:Triquetra-circle-interlaced.svg); Erin Go Bragh font licensed from Iconian Fonts

Figure 6, Triquetra knot illustration, public domain image from Wikimedia Commons (https://commons.wikimedia.org/wiki/File:Vodicka_knot_modified.svg#/media/File:Vodicka_triquetra1.svg); Aon Cari Celtic font free for use in publications

Figure 7, Brock Script font by Dieter Steffmann, free for commercial use (http://www.1001fonts.com/brock-script-font.html)

Chapter 4

Bauer, Michael (2011). *Blas na Gàidhlig: The Practical Guide to Gaelic Pronunciation*. Foillseachadh Akerbeltz. http://www.akerbeltz.eu/books.html

Figure 9, "Gaelic-text-Duibhlinn," Wikimedia Commons. Licensed under CC BY 2.5 via Commons: https://commons.wikimedia.org/wiki/File:Gaelic-text-Duibhlinn.png#/media/File:Gaelic-text-Duibhlinn.png

Figure 10, free Celtic fonts for personal use: Aon Cari Celtic by Cari Buziak (http://www.aon-celtic.com/); Bunchló na Nod by Gaelchló, (http://www.gaelchlo.com/bunnod.html); Erin Go Bragh by Iconian Fonts (http://www.dafont.com/erin-go-bragh.font); Glanchló by Vincent Morley (http://www.fonts2u.com/glanchlo.font); Irish Uncialfabeta by Manfred Klein (http://www.1001freefonts.com/irish_uncialfabeta.font); Kells sd by Steve Deffeyes (http://www.fontsquirrel.com/fonts/Kells-SD); Secretary Hand Ancient, author unknown (http://www.fonts101.com/fonts/view/Celtic/29598/Secretary_hand_ancient)

Chapter 5

Am Bìobull (n.d.). *Leabhraichean an t-Seann Tiomnaidh agus an Tiomnaidh Nuaidh; air an Tarruing o na Ceud Chanainibh chum Gàidhlig Albannach*. Edinburgh and Glasgow: Comunn-Bhìobull Dùthchail na h-Alba (first published in 1801).

Nicolson, Alexander (1996). *A Collection of Gaelic Proverbs and Familiar Phrases*. Edinburgh, Birlinn (first published in 1881).

Glossary Index

A

above 265
again 187, 209, 210
against 258
air 326
Airborne 265
alive 320, 373
always 154, 181, 182, 183
ancestors 193, 384
angel 212, 213, 214
arms 214
army 271
artist 292
atheist 293
athlete 294
awake 321

B

baby 103, 104, 105
bagpiper 311
be 215, 216
beach 133
beautiful 11, 90, 110, 113, 114,
        115, 116, 124, 125, 159,
        322, 323, 324
beloved 4, 59, 60, 64, 65, 74,
        75, 79, 80, 88, 89, 100,
        102, 147, 148, 160, 161
best friend 97, 140
better 371, 392
Bible 52, 147, 148, 153, 171,
        177, 215, 216, 219, 225,
        251, 257

bird 385
bless 325
blessed 217
blessing 218, 325
blood 1, 41, 51
bond 46
book 295
born 385
boy 119, 120, 121, 122, 123,
        124, 125
boyfriend 175
break 357
breath 326
breathe 327
broken 46, 185
brother 98, 99, 100, 101, 102
brown-haired 158, 159
Burns, Robert 34

C

cairn 191, 192, 194
Canada 22
Cape Breton 5, 6, 8, 9, 10, 11,
        12, 13, 20, 23
cat 365
cause 374
champion 267, 288, 291
chance 96
change 372, 394
cheerfulness 365
child(ren) 106, 107, 365
choice 96
Christ 238

circle 250
clan 39, 50, 53
closed 382
confidence 328
conqueror 262
conquer 375
conquest 263
Corinthians 153, 225
country 50, 53, 283
couple 173
courage 328
cousin 83, 84
cure 395

D

Dad 67
Daddy 68
dance 296
dancer 297
dare 376, 377
daughter 19, 108, 109, 110, 111, 126
day 136
death 199, 264, 265, 395
Declaration of Arbroath 29
defender 266
demon 213, 221
Devil 254
die 54, 186
dishonour 264
doctor 298, 304
dog 365
Doomsday 134, 136
door 381
dream 329
drink 378
drug 330
druid 222

E

earth 11
eat 378
end 135, 388
endlessness 344
enemy 375
enough 152, 331
Ephesians 219, 251
essence 388
esteem 370
eternal 127, 128, 129, 162, 201, 202, 205, 206
eternally 128, 129
ever 129, 137, 138
everlasting 130, 223
everything 47, 186
evil 224, 229
Exodus 52
eyes 389

F

faith 49, 131, 225
faithful 333
fame 71
family 41, 42, 43, 44, 45, 46, 47, 48, 49, 50, 51, 53, 54
farewell 23, 24
father 52, 62, 63, 64, 65, 66, 69, 70, 71, 126, 255
fear 364
fearless 279, 364
female 36, 147, 148, 161, 164, 261, 267, 268, 269, 300, 309, 318, 323, 334
fiddler 299
fight 29
fighter 267, 270, 323
fire 247
firefighter 300

first 44, 52
fisherman 301
fist 382
five 116, 123
flame 226, 248
flesh 171, 177
follow 71, 271
fool 334
foolish 335
forefathers 71, 384
foreigner 317
forever 38, 45, 95, 129, 133,
    134, 135, 136, 137, 138,
    154, 184, 198
forgiveness 49
fortitude 384
four 115, 122
Francis, of Assisi, Saint 239
free 25, 26, 27, 28
freedom 29
friend(s) 94, 96, 97, 139, 140,
    389
friendship 141, 142, 157

G

Gael 30, 39
Gaelic expression 439, 71, 70,
    126, 133, 158, 159, 191,
    192
Gaelic song 8, 9, 10, 11
game 388
girl(s) 6, 7, 112, 113, 114, 115,
    116, 124, 125, 158, 159
girlfriend 175
glory 29
God 187, 215, 220, 226, 227,
    232, 242
goddess 256, 228
gold 379, 392

good 229, 230, 337, 338, 339,
    389
good fortune 337
good luck 337, 338
goodness 230
grace 219, 220, 231, 232
grandchild(ren) 81, 82
grandfather 72, 73, 74, 75, 76
grandmother 77, 78, 79, 80
grief 188

H

half 178, 179, 180, 189, 190
hand 187
handsome 120, 121, 122, 123,
    124, 125
happiness 131, 340
harper 303
harpist 303
hate 341, 351
healer 304
healing 342
heart 12, 13, 14, 15, 33, 34, 172,
    183, 184, 197, 198, 200,
    207, 208
Heaven 233
heavy 200
Hector 18, 19
Hell 234
heredity 1
heritage 2
hero 76, 269, 272, 277, 281,
    288, 291, 393
heroine 269
Highlands 34
hole 367
holy 235, 236, 255
Holy Spirit 236, 255
home 380

homesickness 3
honour 29, 52, 53, 61, 69, 191,
    192, 193, 194, 273, 374
hope 131, 225, 343
house 365
hunter 305
husband 143, 145, 163, 165

I

immigrant 312
improvement 337
infant 103, 104, 105
infantry 271
infinity 344
iron 274
island 7, 8

J

Jesus 237, 238, 241
joy 345

K

keep 275
kind 153
kindness 142
know 215, 390, 391

L

land 4, 9, 10, 11, 366
lass 158, 159
late 371
laughter 346, 349, 365
left behind 207, 208
legacy 347
let 27, 378
liberate 26
life 29, 48, 51, 199, 223, 348,
    349

light 326
little 350, 367
live 54, 186
living 207, 208
Lord 239, 257
love 8, 9, 76, 127, 131, 132, 149,
    150, 151, 152, 153, 154,
    157, 162, 167, 168, 169,
    170, 211, 225, 349, 351
loved 146, 155
lover 156, 175, 283, 295
loving 195
loyalty 41, 157
luck 337, 338, 339, 363

M

made in 20, 21, 22, 32
magic 240, 250
man 29, 165, 274, 376, 390
many 379
Mark 172, 177
Mary 241
may 187, 201, 202, 203, 204
meet 187, 210
memoriam 196
memory 191, 192, 195
merciless 280
mercy 275
mermaid 306
middle 92
mighty 352, 355
mirror 389
Mom 56
Mommy 57
mote 253
mother 52, 55, 58, 59, 60, 61,
    66, 126, 241
motto 265, 271
mountains 10

Mum 56
Mummy 57
music 307
musician 308

N

native 1
none 286
nostalgia 3
nothing 382
Nova Scotia 14, 15, 16, 18, 19,
      21, 24
nurse 309

O

ocean 133
oldest 91
one 124, 125, 171, 177
only 172, 242
open 381
our 193, 281, 282

P

pagan 222, 228, 240, 243, 253,
      261
pair 173
Paradise 6244
partner 163, 164, 173, 174
patient 153
patriot 283
peace 201, 202, 203, 204, 205,
      206, 239, 275, 354, 369
performer 310
physician 304
Pictou County 17, 18, 19
pilgrim 313
piper 311
pirate 314
plenty 332

poet 315
powerful 355, 362, 390, 391
pride 356
property 380
prosperity 337
protect 284
protection 250
protector 285
Psalms 215, 216, 257

Q

quiet 368

R

ray of light 326
refreshing 372
regrets 353
related 41
remember 383, 384
rest 201, 202, 205, 206, 357
riches 29
rise 368, 371
rock 97, 394

S

sacred 246, 247, 248
sacrifice 359
sadness 3
sailor 316
saint 249
sanctuary 250
saved 251
Scot 35, 36
Scotland 37, 38, 40, 25, 26, 27,
      32, 33
Scotland the Brave 40
second 286
see 209
serve 284

shepherd 257
ship 18, 19, 367
Ship Hector 18, 19
shoulder 39
shut 381
significant other 173, 174
sink 367
sister 85, 86, 87, 88, 89, 90, 91,
     92, 93, 94, 95, 96, 97
sleep 378
soldier 278, 282, 287, 288
son 18, 70, 117, 118, 119, 120,
     121, 122, 123, 124, 125,
     126
song 8, 9, 10, 11, 24, 34, 40
sorrow 188
soul 178, 179, 180, 189, 190,
     200, 201, 202, 205, 206,
     366
spark 326
spouse 173, 174
still 207, 208, 215, 216
stone 191, 192, 194
stranger 317
stream 394
strong 200, 358, 361, 362
success 337, 363
surrender 373
sweet 380, 385
sweetheart 175, 176
sweetie 168
sword 374

T

teacher 318
thing 379, 382
three 114, 121, 380
tongue 366
tradition 2, 43
traveler 313

trees 10
trinity 259
truth 258, 392
two 113, 120, 124, 125

U

unafraid 364
unbreakable 46
until 133, 134, 187, 209, 210

V

value 370
vegetarian 319
vengeance 289
victory 290
vital spark 326
voice 385

W

war 369
warrior 268, 291, 324
watch 260
water 368
wave 368
wife 144, 145, 164, 166, 380
win 376, 377
witch 261
without 48, 211, 279, 280, 330,
     353, 364, 365, 366, 374,
     393
woman 391
wonderful 40
words 380
world 106, 111, 258
wound 393

Y

youngest 93
yourself 54, 370

Printed in Great Britain
by Amazon